# Parents on Trial

# PARENTS ON TRIAL

## WHY KIDS GO WRONG—OR RIGHT

by

*Reverend David R. Wilkerson*

with

*Claire Cox*

Hawthorn Books, Inc.
*Publishers*          *New York*

PARENTS ON TRIAL

5410

This book is dedicated to Kathryn Kuhlman,
a great woman of God who has had a tremendous
influence on my life.

# Contents

# Parents on Trial

*conclusion* ✗

# Why This Book?

In ten years of helping kids in trouble, I have dealt personally with an average of six hundred teen-age narcotics addicts and a much larger number of delinquents each year. I have come to know them well, and I also have spent considerable time with their parents, out of whose anguish this book has grown. Not a week goes by that I do not counsel hundreds of kids and lecture to an average of four thousand teen-agers groping for the right pathway through life. Many of these youngsters have asked me questions and voiced complaints about their parents.

It hurts me deeply when I cannot give a helpful answer. There have even been times when I have had to walk away from problems of teen-agers, and this is particularly grievous to me. However, in ten years of working with youngsters, a man does gain experience. Some things have become very clear. *child abuse* For example, I have learned that delinquency and drug addiction can strike *any* home, not just impoverished slum dwellings; that outwardly well-adjusted youngsters are not immune to trouble; that the course of a child's life can be favorably *conclusion* ↓

influenced by parents of any educational or economic standing,*if they are not afraid to work at being good parents.*

*Include thesis here* →

*Parents on Trial* is not a digest of answers or formulas. You will not like everything you read. Much of it is not very pretty, and some may be shocking.

*adjust*

The book was born out of my experience, my hopes, and my heartbreaks. I felt I had to write it. In doing so, I hoped not only to provide helpful guidance for parents and those who work with children but also to clarify some aspects of the subject for myself. Since my ministry is dedicated to helping kids stay out of trouble, and once they are in trouble helping them get out of it, I wanted to analyze and study what I had done, where I had been, and where I should be going. Naturally, I hoped, too, that youngsters could gain hope from seeing in print evidence that someone is on their side. Just the knowledge that they have a "friend in court" often makes the difference between a delinquent and an upbeat kid.

Most of all, I hope that discerning parents, parents who really care, will find guidelines, suggestions, and even warnings, and will learn from the mistakes of others. Good parents do not always produce good children, but devoted, dedicated, hard-working mothers and fathers can weigh the balance in favor of decency and the building of moral character. Every word and deed of a parent is a fiber woven into the character of a child, which ultimately determines how that child fits into the fabric of society. I hope those who read what follows will find help in doing a better job as parents, or at least gaining insights into why some kids go wrong and others go right.

*adjust* →

DAVID WILKERSON

New York City, 1967

# Prelude

Two figures sit in the basement of a condemned building huddled in the light of a candle on an overturned orange crate. One of them is a tousle-haired young tough. The other is a minister whose life is dedicated to working with street gangs and addicts—the author of this book. They are talking in the headquarters of a teen-age gang known as the Bishops, composed of a president, a vice president, war lords, a sergeant at arms, and vigilantes. Their girls form an auxiliary called the Bishop Debs and Dolls. The author is talking to the president of the Bishops.

"Do you carry a switchblade or any other weapon?"

"I carry a twenty-two and a zip gun."

"Have you ever been in a rumble?"

"Yeah, we have fights all the time."

"Do you like the sight of the blood?"

"Sometimes. It depends on whose blood it is."

"And you like to fight?"

"Yeah."

"I noticed there were some bayonets around here. Do you fellows actually go out on the street with bayonets?"

"Sure!"

"Why? What would you do with a bayonet?"

"Only about a couple months ago, another gang caught a guy and stabbed him forty times in the chest."

"With a bayonet?"

"Yeah."

"Why do you teen-age boys join gangs in the first place?"

"For protection from other gangs. A lot of people—grown-ups—see us walking down the street in a group and they figure, Here comes a bunch of bums. Well, when they were teen-agers, they probably lived in the country, but in the city, you walk through the street and there is always somebody out to get you, so you walk in groups, for protection."

"Aren't you afraid, son, that somebody will jump out and stick a knife in your back?"

"Yeah, I mean, you know, I don't like to get into things like that, but around our way we got to do it whether we like it or not. We gotta join a clique."

"What about the gangs who throw Molotov cocktails off roofs at cops? Why do they do that?"

"Maybe that's the way they get their thrills. And you know, you have to let the cops know you're not scared of them."

"Most people around the country think that a gang like yours is made up of just a bunch of hoodlums who sleep till noon and dance all day and then go out and fight or take narcotics."

"You don't know that. You don't know what a bunch of *men* we have. A lot of adults call us hoodlums, but they don't realize their own kids are doing the same things, too, behind their backs. When a group of guys get together, you never can tell what they might be cooking up."

"Do you ever think about God?"

"Well, when I'm alone or in bed or when I get in a tight spot, I start thinking, you know, praying."

"Only when you get in a tight spot you start thinking and praying. When the rest of the gangs are around or when you are smoking marijuana or taking narcotics, you don't think about God?"

"No, we don't have the time then."

*scene two*

The author is talking to a young man in a basement coffee-house in Greenwich Village.

"How old are you, son?"

"Seventeen."

"Are you a male prostitute?"

"Yes."

"How long has this been your life?"

"For four or five years."

"Do your parents know what you are?"

"No. It would kill them if they found out."

"Tell me what you think of this life. Are you ashamed of it?"

"It is a disgusting, disgusting life, and teen-agers should never get involved in such a thing. I myself never thought I could bring myself to do such awful things."

"You never thought you would be like this?"

"No, I never realized it would happen to me. A lot of times people say, It could never happen to me; but it can happen and it will happen if you go near these areas where there are homosexuals. It is just like narcotics. You try it once for kicks and it becomes a desperate habit."

"Is this what you would tell teen-agers to keep them from getting involved in this—to stay away from this and not to try it the first time?"

"Yes, don't even try it the first time. You try it once and it becomes a deadly habit. Stay away! I tell teen-agers, stay away!"

"The Bible says there will come a day when people will no longer be ashamed of their sins. Perhaps that day has come."

"There are still a lot of people ashamed of them. There are a lot, like myself, who have a habit of narcotics. I became a prostitute to support that habit."

"From your knowledge, can you say whether a lot of teen-agers are becoming involved with drugs?"

"Yes, in a lot of cities—just about every city along the east coast, the gulf coast, Mexico, Canada, Norway, Sweden, and Denmark. It is not only in our country."

"This is the sin that brought the downfall of Sodom and Gomorrah and the Roman Empire. Will it be the downfall of America?"

"If enough of us teen-agers get hooked on drugs, anything could happen."

# 1

## Six Dead

The sign said "Funeral Chapel," but it was nothing more than a dingy, dirty room in a squalid tenement on New York's Lower East Side. In the closed pine casket were the emaciated remains of nineteen-year-old Bobby Foster, who had died with a policeman's bullet in his heart. Gathered around the casket were perhaps thirty mourners, including Bobby's grieving, bewildered mother, his stepfather, some friends, and a few former addicts I had brought with me to Bobby's funeral.

The occasion gave me a lot to think about, and eventually it started me on a search that has not yet ended. I did not have much time for contemplation and soul-searching during the service—we had to rush through it because the funeral parlor, the cheapest in New York ($300, complete with casket, hearse, and burial), was busy that day. Perhaps it was a fitting kind of farewell for Bobby, who had lived and died in a hurry without learning much about the good things of the world, but

I would have liked time to linger a little longer over our prayerful thoughts for him.

To a casual onlooker, the funeral might have seemed a tragicomic affair. Business was so brisk that day that I had scarcely started my funeral message when the burly owner of the establishment stuck his head through the door and announced, "You'll have to hurry. The hearse has arrived." With that, he swung open the double doors and instructed the driver to remove the casket and get going. Hastily, I closed the service with a short prayer, and the four boys who were to serve as pallbearers approached the casket.

Just as they were about to take hold of what appeared to be bronze bars along the sides of the casket, the funeral director shouted, "No, no, no! Don't touch it!" The "bronze bars" were wooden ornaments painted to look like the real thing, and they would have ripped loose from the cheap pine box if the boys had taken hold of them. The funeral director showed the boys how to lift the casket by the bottom. They placed it on a cart and wheeled it to the long black car waiting at the curb.

Before any of us had time to put on our hats and coats and form an automobile funeral procession, the hearse pulled away. We finally caught up with it near the cemetery, where we found a gum-chewing crew of grave diggers still at work preparing Bobby's grave. They stood by, leaning on their shovels, during the brief graveside service, and the final Amen had hardly been uttered when they set to work again, laughing and joking as they lowered Bobby's coffin into the ground and covered it with dirt. That was the end of Bobby, or so it seemed at the moment, but his ghost has been haunting me ever since.

I said goodbye to Bobby's family and drove off, slowly,

back toward Brooklyn and my work with young addicts and former addicts, homosexuals and street walkers, and other delinquents we hope to save from the fate of the Bobbys of the world. Bobby had been one of our boys once, but we lost him. Why? I brooded about that as I drove through the heavy traffic, and several times I was so lost in thought about him that only the jarring honks of cars behind me made me aware that the light had changed to green.

Bobby's end was a personal defeat for me, a failure, but it may yet signal a kind of victory. In the months since, I have engaged in a search for the reasons why kids go wrong—or right; for explanations for the Bobbys in the world and the disappointments we sometimes encounter in our work with young people. I have been asking many questions, and getting some answers. The truth is often elusive, but I hope to find at least part of the solution eventually, and when I do, the answers may provide a living memorial to Bobby and others like him.

Who was *really* responsible for Bobby's misspent life and his untimely death? I looked back over what I knew of his life, and the lives of other boys we had buried. He was the sixth young addict we had lost to an overdose of heroin, murder, or a policeman's bullet. In a way, I felt I was at least partly responsible for Bobby's death, and for some of the others, too, because we had these boys in our care at the Teen Challenge Center in Brooklyn and then we let them get away. At Teen Challenge, we have cured and rehabilitated scores of young men and women who have been in the clutches of narcotics. Why did we fail with Bobby? More important, why did his parents fail?

Let me tell you a little about Bobby, who was with us for

eight months. He came to us from the gutter after four years
on drugs, during which time he injected as much as fifty
dollars' worth of heroin into his veins in a single day. He had
been in and out of hospitals and treated by psychiatrists, but
he was one of those whom medical science has not been able
to reach. The doctors and psychiatrists could not pierce the
wall that surrounded Bobby, and when he came to us, he was
a bedraggled, lonely, desperate, dejected soul.

After only a few weeks with us, during which time he went
through a painful "cold turkey" withdrawal period, Bobby
gave us cause for hope. There was a smile on his face, he
whistled a tune, and he told everyone he met that he had been
cured of being a junkie. But underneath it all, Bobby proved
to be one of those who come to us begging for care and
treatment but who are never quite able to shake off the
shackles of addiction or the psychological scars dating back
to early childhood. Somehow he felt that even though we had
helped him, loved him, fed him, given him shelter and clothing, provided an education for him, and prayed for him, we
were still against him. Behind his smiles and his whistling,
behind his outward desire to please, there lurked a smoldering
distrust.

I was not as surprised as I might otherwise have been,
therefore, when one day he came to me and said, "David, I
want to visit my old neighborhood just once to see if anyone
there wonders where I've been or still knows me."

This meant only one thing to me. We were in imminent
danger of losing Bobby. The boys and girls we save seldom
want to return to their old haunts, and if they do, it is to find
someone else to help, not to see whether anyone there still
cares about them. It was obvious that Bobby was still hooked

on his old hangouts. He did not want to see his family, but rather the old "friends," the junkies with whom he used to "shoot it up" with heroin.

I advised Bobby not to go, but he said he had to, and as was to be expected, he did not return that night. When he turned up the next day, it was only long enough to pick up his clothes—incidentally, clothing we had given him. I refused to let him go without one final struggle, however, and invited him into my office for a talk.

"Why are you leaving us, Bobby?" I asked.

"It's no use," he replied. "I went to a show, I smoked a cigarette after eight months without one. Then I wanted to shack up with a girl, so I went out and found one. That was no good either, so I said, I'll try just one little shot of heroin to prove I'm over it. When I took that shot, I knew I was still hooked. I could never make it, so I'm leaving. I'm gone."

I tried everything I could think of short of demanding that he stay. You can't win souls by making demands. So I cajoled, I counseled, I prayed, I did everything but weep. It was no use. Bobby had made up his mind. As he turned to leave, I said, "Bobby, unless you learn to love and accept love, you'll never make it. We'll find you in a gutter someday and I'll have to bury you."

Three months passed. Occasionally I ran into Bobby on the street. He said he was living in a hotel with a prostitute who was supporting his habit. I'll never forget how he bowed his head and said, "Davie, I still read my Bible, I pray to God, but I'm hooked. I can't break loose. Don't try to reach inside my heart. No one will ever touch me."

The last time I saw Bobby was only ten days before his funeral. Teen Challenge has converted an old theater on the

Lower East Side into a chapel where we preach to drug addicts and young gang members. We go out into the neighborhood and round up the kids and bring them into the auditorium. On the day I am recalling, eight or ten of the teen-agers had come forward after the service to surrender their lives to God when a breathless youth dashed down the aisle.

"Bobby's outside on the street and he's begging to see you, but he won't come inside," the boy said.

I turned the service over to one of my assistants and went to Bobby. In our work, you go wherever people need help; you don't wait for them to come to you, and you don't turn your back on them even though they may have spurned you. So I went to Bobby. I found him leaning against the wall of the theater building, high on heroin.

"Davie," he said, "I can't make it. I'm going down, down, down. It's like a big slide without any end and I can't stop."

First I became indignant, then furious. I suppose I was angry at our program or even at myself for not having been able to reach Bobby. Perhaps I was wondering why God had not come down and swept Bobby into His Kingdom and remade him. I was angry at Bobby's parents, and at the society that had driven a boy so deep into sin. As a last resort, I decided to try to frighten this boy.

"Bobby," I said, laying my hands on his shoulders, "if you go to church tomorrow evening, get on your knees, open your heart and say, 'Oh, God, I love you; teach me love and help me to love others and trust others, and I surrender my life completely. Take all of these problems out of my mind. Create a miracle for me.' If you ask all of that, God will do it. But, Bobby, if you don't, I'm afraid that you're a dead boy."

For at least thirty seconds, Bobby stood there staring at me, perhaps testing my love and my compassion. Then he raised his hands and let out a yell.

"Then, by God, bury me!" he shouted and ran off.

As the teen-agers say, this experience left me shook. I spent the next three days praying for Bobby's soul and his life. On the fourth day I received a telephone call at home, at one o'clock in the morning. It was one of our workers at the Teen Challenge Center. Bobby Foster had been shot through the heart.

Only an hour before Bobby died, he had encountered John Benton, one of my assistants, in Times Square. John begged Bobby to surrender to God. "Don't you remember what Brother Dave told you?" he asked Bobby. "God loves you. We love you. We're going to help you. Please come back to the center."

All Bobby said was "Forget it."

He went down to the Lower East Side and with a friend stole a car, a 1965 Thunderbird. Bobby was so high on heroin that he let his pal drive, straight through a police roadblock that had been set up in the search for them. The car crashed into a building, and as policemen swarmed around it, Bobby panicked and began to run. An officer fired a warning shot into the air, but Bobby kept on running. Another shot was fired. Bobby fell dead in a gutter.

That is Bobby's story. But is it *really* his story? Isn't there a lot more to it than that? These and other questions kept running through my mind as I drove to Brooklyn after the funeral. I had walked away from six funerals for our former addicts, and I vowed I would not walk away from another without getting some answers. The newspapers and eyewitnesses said it was a policeman who killed Bobby, with a well-aimed bullet through the heart. But did *he* really kill Bobby? I wondered if others were not really responsible. Wasn't it partly our society, which seems to condone so much reckless- ness and lawlessness among our young people? Were not the courts in part to blame because of their laxity in issuing verdicts and sentencing the drug pushers who helped start Bobby down the path to hell? What about the churches? Weren't they partly responsible because of their indecision and lack of compassion, their failure to meet human need and their inability—or reluctance—to rescue young people from poor neighborhoods? And what about the churches that have moved to the suburbs so they won't have to face up to the problems of people crying out for help?

But stronger thoughts than these kept coming back to my mind. I remembered the nights Bobby told me he had spent sleeping in subways and on roofs. The question that kept recurring was, Why didn't Bobby go home? Why did he stay away from his family for two years? I told myself that despite the fact that I had of necessity arrived at certain conclusions about parents, I did not really understand where they had gone wrong—and where society, the school, and the church had gone wrong. I decided to go on a one-man mission to find out, not from theorists, not from specialists, but from the parents themselves. I wanted to talk to the mother and father in the home where Bobby's delinquency had its roots—the mothers and fathers of all our young people. I wanted to start right away, so I decided to begin with Bobby Foster's mother.

When I decided to talk with this mother, I hoped for some real answers to the questions that lay heavy on my heart. I wanted to learn from her and other parents what mistakes they felt they had made. My reason for this was a hope that perhaps with what I learned I could help these parents and others avoid making further mistakes of the same kind and thus help their kids go right instead of wrong.

At the time of Bobby's death, there were eighty-five drug addicts in our care at the rapidly expanding Brooklyn Teen Challenge Center. Also there were gang leaders and members and young prostitutes. I wanted to talk to all their parents and ask them how it all started, why it started, and why they either did not or could not stop it. I wanted to talk to a lot of parents of youngsters at our centers in Chicago, Los Angeles, Detroit, Boston, and other cities, too, because I was sick and tired of double talk and scientific jargon and the wails of mothers and fathers that always came too late.

I was fed up with headlines blaring "What's wrong with our teen-agers?" Wasn't it time to ask rather, "What's wrong with the parents who are producing our problem children?" Perhaps it is parental delinquency we should be more concerned about than juvenile delinquency, I kept telling myself. And so, for that reason, you will find it is with "P.D.," rather than "J.D.," that this book is at least partly concerned.

Now, I am a parent myself and although I make my share of mistakes I like to think that *all* parents are not bad ones —or at least I like to tell myself that *I* am not a bad parent. I did not wish to approach this subject as a preacher on a soap box or as an expert on family relations. No man is in a position to claim to be an authority on parenthood, especially when he, as in my case, has four children still so young that there has not yet been time to prove his effectiveness as a parent. But I did feel that as a gang preacher who had dealt with thousands of teen-agers in trouble, as a father, as a minister of the Gospel, and as an angry young man who is concerned, I had grounds for going to parents in my efforts to find answers that might help the young people who constitute my mission in Teen Challenge.

Our organization was established in 1958 to rescue youngsters from the gutters of New York. Since then, a nationwide ministry has been established, with Teen Challenge centers and programs across the country designed to bring new life and new hope to troubled teen-agers. Possibly of more importance, we work with the upbeat youngsters, too, to help them resist some of the temptations that might put them on the downward path to delinquency. Thousands of these "goodniks," to whom I preach at rallies and other gatherings, set aside nickels, dimes, and quarters from their earnings and allowances and send them to us every week or month to help support our work with less fortunate young people.

Thus, my thoughts about Bobby were in the context of good teen-agers as well as the more than a thousand drug addicts we had helped at Teen Challenge and the ten thousand gang members and juvenile hoodlums I had talked to. I had counseled and spoken to thousands in crusades from coast to coast and overseas. I am sure that my mail, from parents and teen-agers, had been as voluminous as that of any preacher in America or of any counselor, spiritual or secular, on youth problems. My library contained many books expounding many theories about delinquency, the causes and results, but nothing in them satisfied my heart. They did not really answer the questions.

In the years since Teen Challenge came into being, I had been in touch with parents of teen-age—and younger—narcotics addicts, prostitutes, unwed mothers, thieves, rapists, and even killers. For those years I had been helping and rehabilitating delinquents, alcoholic youths, young addicts, homosexually inclined kids, teen-aged beatniks and undisciplined, bored, and broken-hearted sons and daughters. I had walked the lonely streets with them, listening to their complaints against society in general and their parents in particular. My soul had been ignited a thousand times over by the ugly revelations of adult neglect, hostility, and apathy toward children. I had counseled kids in court, on rooftops, in basement hideouts, in fashionable suburbs, at church conferences, rallies, and conventions, in schools and on college campuses, in prisons, and on the beaches.

It seemed to me that more than half of all the teen-agers I had talked to were angry, uncertain, confused, and rebellious to some degree, and I noticed especially that they had lost confidence in an adult society that through blindness, ignorance, and lack of concern had helped to bring about the most critical youth problem in the history of our nation. One had only to look at the facts and figures on juvenile delinquency to feel concern for our society. We will go into those details later, but first I want to tell you about the search that has shaken my faith in parents. Let me assure you that I am not a prophet of doom, I am not a sensationalist, and I certainly am not an expert just sounding off. I am a friend of the troubled young people who have been filling my soul and my mind with stories that have made me blush, cringe, and often weep.

My one-man mission in search of the truth about our teen-age delinquents and their upbringing was to be basically this: I planned to visit the parents of boys and girls who were in our care at our Teen Challenge Center and say, "I've got your son [or daughter] at our center. He is a drug addict [or, she is a prostitute]. I want the honest-to-goodness truth from you. When did you see your child begin to go astray? Where did it all begin? Why do *you* think he went wrong? What could *you* have done to put him on the right path?" I was determined to seek answers to many of the questions that had been raised during my years of work with kids. "I don't want any excuses," I would tell them. "I want answers. I want you to be honest. Tell me the whole story. What is it like to hear for the first time that your own child is a drug addict? What is it like to sit in court and hear him sentenced to prison? What do you feel when you visit him in jail?" I wanted to know what emotions overcome a parent when he asks his child to leave home because he has stolen everything he could lay his hands on to support his narcotics habit. I wanted to know about the sleepless nights—if any—of parents and what these parents would tell other mothers and fathers to spare them from heartache. I wanted to pass along a message right from the heart.

There were many other questions on my mind when I went to see Bobby's mother. Why do apparently "good" parents have problem children? Why do children grow up to steal and kill? What goes wrong to put a teen-ager behind bars? Why do even ministers, judges, and psychiatrists send juvenile delinquents into the world? Who is to blame for the critical and tragic delinquency problem that now exists in this country and in most nations around the world?

Although there is nothing new about blaming parents for juvenile delinquency, it is impossible for us who deal with these youngsters to ignore the fact that parents, in one way or another, must share at least part of the responsibility for the moral landslide among our youth. I wanted to hear from them personally how they felt about this. Admittedly there are parents who cannot help themselves. In New York City alone there are more than eighty thousand deserted women and children. Insane people, according to recent court surveys, now account for nearly 10 per cent of the parents who have children under court jurisdiction. Fathers, some of them psychotic, force their daughters into sexual relationships. Mentally disturbed mothers beat and abuse innocent children. Parents, some of them schizophrenic, neglect and abandon youngsters. But the majority of parents, it is safe to assume, are not psychotic or mentally disturbed; they are simply passive when it comes to the development of their children and somehow cannot manage to love them in a way that is vital if they are to be motivated properly.

When the parents I have encountered in hospital and jail reception rooms and courthouse corridors finally have been forced by the cold facts to acknowledge that their own sons or daughters are thieves or narcotics addicts or in some other deep trouble, I have found their first reaction often is "What did *I* do to deserve this?" whereas they might ask, "What did I do wrong? Where did I fail?" People of a variety of persuasions come up with ready answers, but they all seem to indicate that many parents are frail, out of touch, and unable to cope with the burdens of patience and discipline. I am not a psychiatrist, of course. I am a gang preacher who has spent nearly ten years working with narcotics addicts and other delinquents. What I have learned has not come from books or classroom lectures. I have provided living quarters, farm life, education, and training rehabilitation for drug addicts, paroled teen-agers, prostitutes, and other troubled youngsters. They tell me their problems—how they got started, how they feel their parents influenced their lives, what they hate, and why they are bitter. Sometimes I have been shocked by their comments. Sometimes I have been hurt, too, because I am a parent myself.

These are all things I had gleaned from my talks with young people and from brief encounters with their parents. Now I was going to try to get through to the parents themselves, and I was going to begin with Bobby's mother. As it turned out, I did not even get started with her.

I am sure you have heard of the Iron Curtain and the Bamboo Curtain. Let me tell you about another kind of curtain—the parental curtain of silence. When you begin to seek the truth about why little Johnny or Susie has become delinquent, this curtain drops as surely as the curtain that falls at the end of a Broadway play.

# 2

## "But I Was a Good Mother!"

If weeping is any gauge, the flow of tears Bobby's mother had shed at his funeral indicated that she loved him dearly. Compassion and a sense of guilt were indicated when, as the final prayer was recited over his coffin, she screamed, "Bobby, Bobby, Bobby, my baby, my son! God forgive me, God forgive me!" She gave the impression that she blamed herself for her boy's untimely end at the age of nineteen.

What I now learned from Bobby's mother, and learned later from the parents of other young people in trouble, is that the words unleashed at the height of grief and anguish are not necessarily repeated or even remembered in the more tranquil moments that follow. As it turned out, Bobby's mother, like so many I have encountered, did not really blame herself at all. She wanted forgiveness, it is true, but for Bobby, not herself. And she blamed everyone who had ever figured in Bobby's life—*except* herself.

Bobby's mother became but the first of many to refuse to open her heart. Her silent curtain covered only herself—her own guilt. She wanted to blame everyone—the neighborhood, the school, the people who lived next door, the police, Bobby's friends, the church—everyone but herself. After all, hadn't she given him life? She had laid down the "right" rules for him, but Bobby had had bad friends and they had led him astray. His teachers didn't like him. His Sunday school teacher complained that he was unruly and disrespectful in class. The "nice" kids in the block did not want anything to do with him. But it was not *her* fault. Mother wanted no part of the blame. Hers was a good home, neat, comfortable, and containing "everything a child could want." The other children had turned out all right, so clearly the fault lay entirely with Bobby.

"If I had been to blame," she told me, "I wouldn't have had two good children. I had a bad one because he got in with the wrong crowd."

Beyond that, Bobby's mother would not go. The curtain was falling. It closed completely after one further word of accusation. She pointed at me.

"*You* lost Bobby for us all!" she cried. "If you had been a little more patient, if you had tried a little bit harder, he would have been saved."

This confused mother was what I have come to call the buck-passing parent. She had not stopped to wonder what would have happened if *she* had been more patient, tried a little bit harder. Unfortunately, she had no insight whatever into the situation. She saw no relationship between Bobby's delinquent behavior and the fact that she was widowed two months before he, the youngest of her three children, was born, and that she had had to leave him in the care of others during the days when she went out to work. As soon as Bobby was old enough to look after himself, she stopped arranging for someone to tend to him. Then she married again. Her new husband was a nice enough man, but by the time he came into Bobby's life, there was not much he could do for the boy, and he really did not try very hard. Bobby already was an independent, unruly soul who spurned attention and affection. Was any of this his mother's fault? Not in the least. She blamed his teachers, his friends, the cop on the beat. For herself, there was only self-praise because she had been able to keep her family together.

I was not discouraged by this first interview, however. It was only the beginning of my search. My next stop was our theater chapel on the Lower East Side, where I had an appointment with the father of Sammy Rogers. Sammy had been a drug addict for twelve years and now he was studying for the ministry. He had been rescued by Teen Challenge and was doing just fine. I was certain that Sammy's father would be honest with me, not like Bobby's mother. After all, Sammy was out of danger. There had been no funeral, no grief. He was very much alive, and his father was proud of him. Certainly, I told myself, Mr. Rogers will be willing to take a look at the past and try to give me some of the answers I am seeking.

When I reached the theater, I greeted Mr. Rogers. We sat in the back of the empty auditorium and chatted for a while about Sammy and how well he was doing. Then I took out my portable tape recorder and turned it on. "The first question I want to ask you is this: Please tell me honestly, simply, why did your son become a drug addict?"

The curtain fell. Mr. Rogers stared at me in complete innocence and replied, "Reverend, I can tell you in two words—bad friends. *They* led him astray."

Then came a torrent of words that made the father's silence on the crucial question seem deafening. "We loved him. We took him to church. We gave him everything he needed. We did everything for him. After he started on drugs, we used to argue over which of us would go into his bedroom to see whether he was still alive. We lived through hell and mortification. Since he has been reformed, we have sat down and discussed all the problems, objectively, and we have decided that it just wasn't our fault. Sammy just ran with the wrong kids."

Astonishment stunned me into silence, but not for long. I asked, "Mr. Rogers, isn't there *anything* you can tell me about what you and your wife might have done wrong in raising Sammy? Can you look back at any failure in your raising of him, any little incidents, especially when he was very young and in the early teens?"

Without hesitation, the father shook his head, smiled, and said, "Reverend, we just cannot see what we did wrong. We did everything we could for our boy. I tell you it was his friends."

I snapped off the tape recorder and put it away. This was enough information—or lack of it—for one day, but it was enough for me to think about for quite a while. Mr. Rogers was right, as far as he went in his thinking. It *was* Sammy's friends who had led him astray. But why had Sammy run with the kind of teen-agers who were a bad influence on his life? Home is where we learn to set standards and develop our value systems. Perhaps Sammy's parents were delinquent in not giving this kind of instruction or in failing to set the right kind of example. When Sammy began running with the wrong gang, what did his parents do about it? They simply scolded him; they did not offer him any alternatives. I have known many parents who have, often at great sacrifice, moved to a different neighborhood when they saw their children headed the wrong way. The Rogers family could have moved, but it was *convenient* for the parents to stay where they were. They paid dearly for this convenience.

I felt real compassion for the parents of both Sammy and Bobby, for they really did not know what they were doing or saying and they had no insights into themselves or the problems with which they were fumbling. After all, I told myself, parenthood is just about the toughest, most important job in the world, yet it is performed almost entirely by amateurs. Nearly all of us are at least to some degree bewildered on the day we take our firstborn in our arms for the first time and embark on the perilous career of child-rearing. As far as society is concerned, marriage is the only prerequisite for parenthood, and we are getting married at ever younger ages, so that many of us are producing children when we are scarcely more than children ourselves.

When you consider the importance of parenthood, it is amazing to realize that there is no such thing as a training school for the parents of the Bobbys and Sammys and all the upward of four million American children born each year, or a college degree in the science of parenthood. As a matter of fact, there are surprisingly few courses or even books that can really help us learn the necessary skills and acquire the understanding we should have. We fumble along, left largely on our own to have babies, wanted or unwanted, with only helpful

hints from Dr. Spock, the Children's Bureau, and our neighborhood pediatrician to guide us. Other than those somewhat
makeshift aids, our only preparation for providing the world
with tomorrow's citizens—for better or for worse—has been
our own experience of having been children ourselves.

What do the so-called experts say? On my return to my
office after talking to the parents of Sammy and Bobby, I
looked through a few books, magazine articles, and newspaper
clippings on the subject. Even Dr. Benjamin Spock himself, in
his advice to parents in a newspaper interview, acknowledged
that "most people learn to be parents by being children. . . .
All the time a person is a child he is both a child and learning
to be a parent. After he becomes a parent he becomes predominantly a parent reliving childhood." This obviously is a
rather inadequate approach to efforts to improve on past
generations, and by the time *our* children are grown, it is too
late for us to correct our mistakes. I guess you could say that
parenthood is the only on-the-job training program from
which one is dismissed as soon as he completes the course!

This is what I call potluck parenthood, and some of its
results are to be found today in our jails, mental hospitals, and
street gangs; in our high rates of school dropouts, divorce, and
illegitimacy; and in a constant rise in narcotics addiction,
alcoholism, and homosexuality. To be sure, more "goodniks"
than "badniks" are emerging from our American homes,
where love and mutual regard and trust have made it possible
for parents and children to grow together. If there is a thread
that has run through my own experience with parents and
children it is the thread of love in homes that have produced
our "goodniks" and the thread of neglect or disinterest in
those that have turned out delinquents.

It has been said that love is what makes the world go around. It certainly keeps the home fires burning. I suggest that if the parents of Bobby and Sammy had loved them *enough,* and *shown* their love, the stories of these two boys would have been quite different. I can name hundreds of other delinquents I have counseled who have eventually been able to trace the start of their lives of crime and irresponsibility back to the day they found out that their mother or father, or both, had no love for them. And if the youngsters are to be believed, there is a heartbreaking absence of love in many homes of the wealthy, the intelligent, the so-called upper crust of society, as well as in the poorer environments.

Nicky Cruz, child of the streets, jolted me into my first real awareness that so many homes are without love, and being without love, are destroying the very souls they create. Nicky is an associate of mine now. You could not find a more gentle, loving person. But when I first met him, he was a wild animal, a potential killer, filled with hate. Why? It began when he was only four years old, standing on the back porch of his family's home listening to a group of women chatting over tea with his mother. There Nicky heard one searing sentence that was branded on his heart, leaving a scar he will carry all his life.

"We did not really want Nicky," his mother said. "I wish he had never been born."

Nicky, of course, did not fully understand what he had heard, but he understood enough to weep—and it was sixteen years before he shed another tear. During those sixteen years, he ran away from home and lived like an animal until Teen Challenge workers convinced him that there was another way to exist. He finally cried, like a baby, the day I asked him to surrender his life to God and learn the true meaning of love.

Another gang leader who comes to mind was a boy we'll just call Joe. Our friendship began on a park bench in the Fort Green housing project area in Brooklyn. I could hardly believe what he told me that muggy July night as we talked about problems, mainly his.

"Mom *likes* me to be in the gang," Joe said. "It gives her prestige in the housing project. Everybody is afraid of her because she can get her 'boys' after them. She doesn't want me to kill anyone, but she likes people to look up to her, and that's part of the reason I'm in the gang."

Clearly the first thing to do to help Joe was to get him away from his mother. I have learned that this is often the first step we must take, and sometimes it is necessary also in helping youngsters from more affluent suburban families. So I not only took Joe away from home but moved him to a country place in Pennsylvania. I took him away from a mother who sought dubious status by nurturing criminal instincts in her son. Joe became a Bible scholar and vowed that he was through with the life of a gang fighter—forever.

The day eventually came when Joe felt strong enough to go home and face the world away from our shelter and guidance. He went with the hopes and prayers of all of us. But he could not fight off the wicked elements of the city, a neighborhood full of hoodlums, and a mother with an ugly character all at once. With his mother's support, he might have made it. As it happened, his old gang—the Phantom Lords—wanted him back, and they were determined to get him. For weeks he ran from the gang, dodging its bullets and taunts and ignoring daily harassments. One day a slug found its mark in his left leg. Threatening signs were smeared on the wall outside his apartment. His mother pleaded hysterically with him, "Get back in the gang. Don't be such a coward. They will kill *me!*" she cried.

Defeated, by the gang, by his mother, and by himself, Joe returned to the life he had vowed never to resume. Seldom have I been as shocked or angry as I was the day I picked up a newspaper to find Joe on the front page, indicted with four other young men for manslaughter.

A few months later, his mother telephoned me. She was weeping. "Please help my boy," she pleaded. This mother, who was as responsible as any one person could possibly be for the tragedy of her son's life, was asking someone else to help him. She did not ask, What can *I* do to help my boy? No. She wanted someone else to rush to his side now that it was too late for anyone to do very much.

All I could do at this point was to write to Joe, and somewhere in my files I have a number of very touching letters he sent me during his five years in prison. Most of them repeated over and over again that he did not really blame his mother, that he had forgiven her. Every line he wrote in this vein was an exposure of his own heart, subconsciously placing the blame on his own mother.

Would Bobby have blamed his mother if he had lived and gone to jail? I wonder. And the next time I see Sammy Rogers I am going to ask him if his father gave me the "right" answers as far as Sammy is concerned.

I decided to turn to the kids themselves to find out what they thought of their upbringing. I had been unsuccessful so far in my efforts to reach the parents of youngsters in trouble, and I thought that I should go back to the boys and girls I had

been working with and ask them what they thought was wrong
—and right—about their parents and their upbringing. I
hoped that might open some new avenues of investigation. At
least it was worth trying.

# 3

# Why Some Kids Have Given Up on Parents

"I've always blamed my mother for the trouble I've been in because I figured when I was just a little kid I didn't know any better and she should have done something about it."

This was tough little Tony talking. While his parents bickered their way to divorce, he was learning how to throw firecrackers at people. One day he dropped a cherry bomb from a roof onto a pedestrian's head, inflicting serious injuries, and was sent to a juvenile detention home. As is too often the case, the institution proved to be a preparatory school that toughened him for more serious crime. When he came out, he joined a street gang; he fought, stole, smoked marijuana, and, finally, mainlined heroin.

"I hated my mother," Tony told me. "Hate alone made me blame everything on her for the way I lived. After the divorce, my mother began to drink and bring men home, sometimes during the day. She would send me out to play without even giving me lunch.

"I learned how to steal when I was only seven because I would see the other kids with roller skates and bicycles. My parents couldn't afford to buy me things like that, so I used to beat up the other kids and take their skates and things. The cops would come over and I would have to go to court. My mother always promised to see that I was a good boy, but she was too busy for anything like that."

Tony told all of this to me after I had tried in vain to see his mother. I had sweated my way up five flights of dimly lighted stairs in a reeking tenement only to have his mother slam the door in my face. She wanted nothing to do with her boy or anyone who was associated with him. "He's no good," she said. "He'll never be any other way."

So all I can tell you is Tony's side of the story. He is not bitter any more now that he is deeply involved in Teen Challenge, trying to help other youngsters who have been in trouble, but he wanted me to pass along this advice for parents: "When a kid tries to talk to his mother or father, the parents should always find time to listen to what the kid has to say and try to understand him and love him. And they should always pay attention to what a kid's doing, always know where he is and who he's hanging out with.

"I read an old saying someplace. It went, 'If you tell me who your friends are, I'll tell you what kind of person you are.' This is true. Parents should know a lot about the neighborhood they live in. If it's a bad neighborhood, they should either move out or keep an extra eye on the kids. It's pretty easy to fall in with the wrong bunch because there's so much temptation, most of it fun to a kid.

"It's up to the mother and father to love their kids and teach them to be good. Mothers and fathers should understand their children and listen to them because kids aren't stupid even though they may be young. In other words, don't sleep on a kid."

I think this is pretty good advice. As I went along, I was amazed at some of the thoughts expressed by these kids. Their language was not eloquent, but their ideas surely were. "Give us a chance," they all seemed to cry out. "Give us a chance!"

John was another boy I learned something from. He was a high school dropout who had cherished hopes of going to college some day, but his home life was so miserable that he just stopped trying. He threw his books into a trash can on his way home from school one day and never returned to class again. Then he began mixing with street toughs. I guess it was inevitable that he should become a narcotics addict. He was in pitiful condition when one of our workers found him, but his will was strong and we have every hope that he is not only going to be all right but will get to college eventually.

John refused to tell me where I could find his parents. He wanted nothing more to do with them because he was afraid they might drag him down again. Unlike Tony, John blamed his father almost entirely for his troubles. He had very little to say about his mother. "I blame my father most of all," he said, "because I used to go to him all the time and tell him about how I wanted to become an engineer, but he never paid any attention. He didn't want to be bothered. Neither of my parents ever cared about me or showed me any love. I had nobody."

Lewis bounced into my office at this point. I say "bounced" because in his newfound exuberance that is the only way he ever moved around. I asked John if he would like to stay and listen to Lewis's story, and he readily agreed. Lewis is a little fellow, but he has made up for his small stature with more pep and ambition than we usually find in our boys. He's the hardest worker we have, but he was not always this way. Only a few months ago he was the little Napoleon of the street gangs, a title he won with his fists, which he started swinging with a vengeance at age fourteen.

"Because I was small," he told John, "people started picking on me and calling me a measly runt, and I couldn't do anything about it because I was too scared. But when I got older, I felt all the time that I had to fight somebody to be something, like the leader of a gang maybe. I fought with a guy to become vice president of a big gang. I beat him up three times and once I knocked him out."

Lewis came from the worst kind of slum environment, the sort that breeds many of New York City's young criminals. Several years ago, a group of sociologists concluded after a special study that a relatively small number of homes produced most of the city's juvenile delinquents. "Crime-breeding families" was the label given to these clusters of humanity living in near destitution in crowded tenements. This was the kind of family Lewis finally escaped from. His father drank and beat his mother. Once the father threw a knife at her, cutting her hands severely when she held them up to protect her face.

"I ran away," Lewis said. "When I came back four days later I thought my father was going to beat me up for sure, but he was at work. It was pay day and when he came home he was drunk and started another fight with my mother. He started kicking her and punching her and I yelled at him to stop. He hit me and banged my head against the wall. I picked up a broom and hit him on the head and made him bleed. He kicked me and when my mother tried to make him stop, he slapped her. Then all of a sudden he stopped and picked me up and said he was sorry. When he woke up the next morning, he did not remember what had happened. At least that's what he said."

Lewis is worried about his younger brother and sister, who are still at home. They are having problems at school just as he did before he dropped out, and they have been playing hookey a lot. "I used to fight with the teachers, too," Lewis recalled. "I used to fight with the girls and break windows. I even got into a fight with the principal once."

"Why?" I interrupted to ask.

"Well, I don't know," he replied. "I guess I was no good in school from the beginning."

"Do you blame your father for all your trouble?"

"In a way, yes. Years back he used to be nice. He would go to work and bring back money for my mother to buy food and clothes for her and us kids. I don't know what started him drinking. I guess it was his friends. He just hung out with the wrong friends and kept on drinking.

"Then I became just like him. He let me smoke when I was fifteen and he let me drink, too, so I started drinking at home and outside. I kept on drinking and then I went to pills and then marijuana."

It takes money to support this kind of life, so Lewis started stealing and robbing to pay for it. He was arrested twice for robbery and mugging, once to get money to go to the movies. "It was pretty boring at home," he says now, "but I had a lot of fun in the street. All my friends were outside, so I went outside, too. That would have been okay, I guess, if I'd had the right friends. Parents should make sure their kids have the right friends, good friends, and teach them the right way to live, not the wrong way. They should keep kids away from smoking and drinking and teach them right from wrong."

I told Lewis and John a little about my own boyhood, in a Pennsylvania farm community. My father was never a wealthy preacher and my mother had to stretch every dollar to make sure we had the food and clothes we needed. Home was a place where Dad was a real man and all of us respected him. He wore the pants in the family. He was obeyed and he taught us right from wrong and how to work, love, live, and be honest. Dad was a stern disciplinarian, but he always let us know he loved us after every session of woodshed therapy. "As long as you live under my roof," he declared, "you will obey me." And nobody argued because we had learned he was acting out of love for us.

It was Mom who really made our house a home. Her arms were always open when we came in with scratched knees, crying. She scrubbed, baked, sewed, cleaned, washed and ironed, wept and prayed, and she loved and cared. Mom was a mind-reader, too, as so many wise mothers are. When I came home scared to death as a result of some minor infraction I had committed, she would say, "All right, David, come here," and I knew I had to tell her what I had been up to, because if I didn't *she* would tell *me* where I had been and what I had been doing.

We had no television, no basement recreation room, no motorboat, and no money for hobbies, but we had something few homes have today, and that was peace. Mom and Dad and all the kids sat around in the evening and sang songs and pulled taffy and popped popcorn and had a wonderful time. Not a day passed without a family Bible and prayer session.

Lewis and John sat wide-eyed as I told them about my family life when I was growing up, and about how my mother or my father would take me aside for a little talk whenever they saw me getting out of line.

"Did your mother ever do that?" I asked Lewis.

"Well, she did sit down and talk to me once in a while," he said, "but there was always something, a barrier or something that made me turn my back on my parents. She didn't have any punch. Neither did my father."

That is the way it went, in interview after interview with youngsters at our center. They could almost always pinpoint the blame for their troubles—mother, father, or both. But I simply could not get through to the parents. It took the insight of youth, the youth of Jimmy, a once-surly kid who spent more time in the street and in jail than in his own bed until he came to us, to enlighten me further on delinquent parents.

"I didn't have much to say to my family," he said. "You know, I think a lot of times parents are living two lives, if you understand what I mean. They want to be good parents and they want to bring up their children right, try to love their children and everything, but at the same time they're thinking a lot about their own lives. I can remember when I was very young some of the things my mother did were, I thought, very wrong. Even though I was very young, and maybe she didn't realize it, they still stuck in my mind."

"What were some of those things?" I asked.

"Drinking, for one. She used to drink. You have a high standard for your mother, and to see her do things wrong at parties or places like that is a shock to a kid. In my eyes, she should have been a wonderful person, and she just wasn't. She did so many things I didn't like and they stuck in my mind.

"I think a person's family should be his whole life and everything should be done with the children in mind. I don't mean that a kid should be babied and pampered, but home should be a place with real family life where everyone does things together. The kids ought to feel that they are a part of their parents and their parents are a part of them. With that kind of life, nobody turns somewhere else for fun because they have it at home. Also, parents shouldn't say one thing and then do another. A child looks at life the way his parents live it."

I had to end the interview, much as I hated to, because I had received a call to visit our rehabilitation center for girls, just down Clinton Avenue from our Brooklyn center. One of the young women we had rescued had arrived from Bible school for the week end and she had promised to tell me her side of the story of her family life. Most of the young people we work with are boys, but we have had an increasing number of girls come to us for help. One of these was Irene, a pyschiatric nurse who started taking drugs when she was twenty-two. I should say here that although our organization is called Teen Challenge and has a program designed basically for teen-agers, we do not turn away older or younger people who need guidance. In Irene's case, her trouble went deep into her childhood, and emotionally she was little more than a teen-ager when she came in begging us to save her because nothing else had worked.

I was delighted to see Irene again and noted how well she looked. Her once blotchy skin was clear. She wore an attractive summer dress and her hair had been reeently curled—

quite a contrast from the unkempt, sad creature who had shuffled across our doorstep only a year before.

"How is school coming?" I asked her.

"Oh, Brother Dave, it is just wonderful. I'm really enjoying being back in school again. They tell me I should make a good missionary now that I've gotten rid of all my own demons."

We chatted a few minutes and I told Irene about my search for what is wrong with today's parents. She sympathized with me for the frustrations I had encountered and assured me it was no easy task to deal with the parents of delinquents. I asked Irene about the roots of addiction and other delinquency and added a question I had wanted to ask her before: "Why would a girl like you, with a career in nursing, knowing all the hazards, want to start taking drugs?"

"That's a very hard question to answer," she admitted. "I know I was determined to destroy myself in some way. I just didn't have any real purpose or goal. I think that's about the only answer I could honestly give."

I asked Irene about her childhood. She was one of eight children in a lower-middle-class home. Her father was "very lax, very ineffectual," she said. "Discipline wasn't in his vocabulary at all. If there was any disciplining to do, it was done by my mother, but for me there was no discipline. I was the youngest of the eight. Until I was twelve years old, I was at my mother's side almost all the time. I was the baby. The relationship between my mother and father was very erratic, and there was no consistent discipline in the family for the others."

When she was twelve, Irene's mother died, and the home "sort of fell apart," with an older sister looking after the seven other children. Irene found it hard to adjust to losing her mother, and if discipline in the family had been inconsistent before, now there was none at all. As far as she was concerned, however, the damage had been done by her overindulgent mother, and no amount of discipline now would have done her any good.

"Discipline should start when you are a baby, and it should involve the little things as well as the big ones," she said. "If you learn about the small things, the big ones come easier. All I had to do when I was little was to cry and I got my own way, whereas a good spanking would have done the trick. Discipline is so important that I think once it is started everything else sort of falls into place. It is a sort of cornerstone on which you build your life."

We talked a few minutes longer and then I went back to my office, to think about the conversations of the day, and to go through some of the material I had been collecting in connection with my research. Whenever I came across a newspaper item or a magazine article dealing with parents and discipline I tossed it in the back of a desk drawer. Now the drawer was about full, and I decided to see what was there. To my pleasant surprise, I found that researchers had uncovered basically the same kinds of feelings that had been expressed by the young people I had been interviewing in an admittedly unscientific way.

For example, Science Research Associates, in a report on a survey of fifteen thousand teen-agers, found that discipline was the chief source of friction between parents and children. The youngsters said they wanted to be made fully aware of the reason for any punishment and to know that it was being carried out for constructive reasons, not just to hurt or humiliate them.

Ninety per cent of the teen-agers said that they looked to

their parents for instruction in what was right and wrong but that their parents did not always fill this need. Only about half went to their parents with their personal problems, and the same number said they did not think their parents understood their problems. Quite a few indicated that they felt their parents withheld advice because they thought the youngsters did not want it.

In one way or another, the kids I had been talking to had been saying much the same thing. Perhaps I was really getting somewhere in my firsthand research. It was not very expert, but I seemed to be getting to the point.

I continued reading. There was an item from *The Sign,* a national Roman Catholic magazine, which listed the seven biggest problems of teen-agers as gleaned in a survey of eight thousand high school seniors. The number one problem for the boys was trouble at home. For the girls, the pains of adolescence were first, with the home situation second. Other problems listed by boys were sex instruction, steady dating, social conformity, drinking, choice of college, and cars. In discussing their home situations, many of the boys complained that they seldom saw their fathers, who were too busy making money, playing golf, or reading newspapers.

"I hope that when I get married and begin to raise a family I'll have enough brains to realize that being a good father means something more than just making money," one boy said.

I was particularly interested in the magazine's comments on drinking, which was a problem in the homes of many of the youngsters I had talked with. "It's tragic," *The Sign* said, "how many boys mention the problems created by their parents' drinking and the unbearable situations at home that result."

As for the girls, the survey found that they tend to be troubled in the area of obedience, in their compliance with regulations and restrictions imposed by parents who were urged to put their feet down firmly when they discovered their daughters running around with boys who bought them liquor.

Teen-agers have just about been surveyed to death, but if you will bear with me, I would like to add still another set of conclusions: A Gallup poll showed that most teen-agers who answered a question on the causes of excessive teen-age drinking and use of goofballs and dope replied that their parents were not strict enough and their home life was bad. The second most frequently given cause was a desire to do what their friends did and conform to the crowd. Other reasons were to show off and act grown up, to try something new "for kicks," to escape from reality. Dope is easy to get, they also said, and besides, they have nothing else to do.

A Wisconsin boy was quoted as saying that when teen-agers take dope it is their way of trying to show their parents that they have a problem and it also is a good way to get even with their parents.

Many kids criticized parents for telling them they shouldn't do things and then doing them themselves. Twenty-five per cent thought adult behavior was worse than theirs and an equal number thought it was better.

That's about enough time to spend in "surveyland," I decided, and I turned to a booklet by Dr. Norman Vincent Peale, "How to Be Young and Enjoy It." Dr. Peale had learned from the headmistress of a girl's school that 75 per cent of her students found it was difficult to talk with their parents. He told about a letter he had received from a fourteen-year-old girl, saying, "For the past three months I have been trying to get along with my mother, but it is impossible. She gripes and nags and makes me miserable. I so often feel depressed, and when I try to tell her about it, she laughs and makes fun of me. I really need your help."

An eighteen-year-old wrote him, "It just seems as if I can't talk to my mother and father because they never understand me."

From another youngster came the complaint, "I am 12 years old and my parents don't understand me. Mom and Dad can spank me or keep me in the house all day, but it doesn't help. They can't seem to understand what just explaining things can do."

And finally, a boy wrote, "I am a teen-ager. Just how in the world can I get my mother and father to see my point of view?"

Dr. Peale looked at the situation first from the parental point of view, suggesting that young people begin by thinking of their parents as people—the father as a man, the mother as a woman, but he added: "Of course, the problem isn't one-sided. It is pretty tragic when a parent is so tired or busy that he or she cannot welcome an exuberant young person who is filled with life and enthusiasm and talk with that teen-ager at the time when he or she wishes to blurt out all the joy or heartache that is on his mind. Lots of parents are actually disrespectful of children and do not treat them as people. They must learn that a young person is a person, not a child.

"I cannot emphasize too strongly that a parent can understand a child and a young person can understand a parent if each will think of the other as people and treat each other with respect, politeness, and love."

I was reminded of a conversation that was relayed to me

involving a man who told a friend, "We lost our first child." The friend replied, "I didn't know she was dead!" "Oh," the father responded, "she isn't *dead*. I was too busy." By then it was too late for him to have time.

The case of a seventeen-year-old boy also comes to mind. He was under arrest for juvenile delinquency and had been sent to a detention home to await trial. One night the boy went berserk. He managed to wrench a radiator pipe loose, break all the windows he could reach, and then dash about brandishing the pipe for four hours. It took tear gas to finally end his rampage. Under questioning, this boy explained in one short sentence why he had gone on his spree. "I had nothing to lose," he said. That was his way of declaring, "I have already lost the only thing that could have kept me, and that was my home."

I read stories such as this in our newspapers with distressing frequency. There is account after account of young people who go berserk, of kids who start taking drugs, and of other juvenile infractions. Their homes had not held them in check. I am thinking now of a girl who came up to me one night in a restaurant. She said she knew who I was and wanted to talk to me.

"I'm the saddest girl in town," she said. "I work and then I go home and have nothing to live for. I go home determined to keep my parents from killing one another and to keep my brother from beating up my sister."

There were tears in her eyes as she added, "We used to have such a happy home. My father went to church and we all got along fine. Then something happened to my father. He just got tired of it all. He became bored with my mother and they began to fight. He started drinking and she went out with other men. Now I hate my home but I feel I have to be there to keep my mother and father from killing each other."

I wonder how long she will feel that way. I wonder when she will decide that home is just too much and leave. In my ministry among young people, I have found this kind of story amazingly often. Youngsters give up on their homes and their parents, then they turn to the herd, the gang, the streets, and crime. Their parents are too wrapped up in their own concerns to notice.

The young son of such a man eventually was brought before a judge to be sentenced for forgery. The judge had been a friend of the boy's father, a noted lawyer.

"Young man," the judge said, "do you remember your father, that father whom you have disgraced?"

"I remember him well," the young man replied. "When I went to him for advice or companionship, he would say, 'Run away, boy, can't you see I am busy reading?' Well, Your Honor, my father finished reading his book, and here I am."

A famous prison warden has made a comment that is appropriate to include here. When James A. Johnston, for many years warden of Alcatraz Prison, that forbidding penal institution on a rock in San Francisco Bay that was closed a few years ago, was asked to comment on the crime rate in our country, he said:

"The crime problem is the boy problem, and the finest prisons in the world are only monuments to neglected youth."

# 4

---

# The "Hidden" Delinquents

The evidence gathered so far in my search for the "facts" about the family life of delinquents may seem to indicate that young troublemakers are a problem mainly in the slums. Don't make the same mistake I did by jumping to that conclusion, for that most certainly is not the case. The number of youngsters being labeled delinquent across the country is rising toward the million-a-year mark, and an ever-increasing proportion of them are coming from the "right" side of the tracks.

When I began my work with delinquent boys and girls on the sidewalks of New York, I was naïve enough to think that juvenile crime and hoodlumism were solely a big-city problem, that teen-age narcotics addicts, thieves, and vandals came only from tenements and poverty-ridden homes. I was to learn how wrong I was when I began to receive calls for help from the so-called privileged and overprivileged neighborhoods. These requests come with increasing frequency, and we have even given shelter at our Teen Challenge centers to young people from the more affluent segment of our society. I will tell you in a later chapter about one of them, a young man named Larry, who had a part-time father and then flopped at fatherhood himself.

Meanwhile, if you want to know "how the other half lives," as far as delinquency is concerned, let me assure you that in some ways it does not offer much improvement over what happens in our deprived neighborhoods. The kids who get emotional short shrift at home are as numerous in suburbia and exurbia as anywhere else—possibly more so because their parents have more money to spend escaping from their responsibilities.

Parental delinquency exists in all segments of our culture. The youngsters who come from middle-class and wealthy urban, suburban, and rural areas can be as miserable as any others, and often are. I have seen, read, and heard enough about them to know that the amount of money in the family bank account, the size of the house, and the number of cars and television sets are not reliable barometers of the effectiveness of a parent who rears children who go right. It is the amount of love and understanding and the time for showing that love that is the gauge.

What I learned, and admittedly only recently, that may surprise others as much as it did me is that the statistics on juvenile crime tell only part of the story—how small a part we may never know, for a wave of "hidden delinquency," apparently of serious proportions, is sweeping many good neighborhoods. In "Profile of Youth," published in 1967 by the Senate Subcommittee on Employment, Manpower and Poverty, statistics were given on a report that showed the number of undetected delinquents was about three times the number of youngsters who were arrested. The report further indicated that most of the hidden delinquents were members of middle- and higher-income families. In most such cases, youngsters apparently are able to avoid the stigma of criminal records— on paper, that is—because their fathers can afford lawyers to convince policemen and judges that childish "pranks" are to be forgiven and forgotten.

One case, and one that received considerable prominence in the press, is a good example of the kind of parental delinquency I am talking about. The parents of the youngsters involved in this shameful incident make my blood boil. In Oklahoma City in the summer of 1965, a fifteen-year-old girl was trapped in the back seat of a blue convertible on a lonely country road. There one teen-age boy calmly instructed six of his friends on how to molest the girl. He apparently thought she would never tell anyone.

"Don't throw cigarette butts on the ground," he said. "Don't tear the girl's undergarments. Don't leave marks on her throat."

Later the girl, a high school student visiting from another city, told police that all seven of the boys raped her. Some of them came from affluent families. The father of one was a former president of the State Bar Association, the father of another a well-known attorney. One of the boys was a physician's son. The son of a prominent prohibitionist and perennial political candidate also participated.

Now here is the part that shocked me the most. The father of one of these boys went to the aunt of the raped girl and asked that charges be dropped because *"Boys will be boys. Why ruin their reputation and your own?"*

When the County Prosecutor, Curtis Harris, heard that this father had referred to the mass rape as "just a boyhood prank," he declared, "When a father has that attitude, no wonder a boy will do these things, because the parent himself condones it."

Harris at that time disclosed that sex clubs had been operating in the Oklahoma City schools and that there had been a dozen other recent youth rape cases that had not been publicized because the parents of the victims preferred not to press charges. "The parents want the authorities to do something about it," he said, "but without their willingness to testify, there is nothing we can do."

I wonder how many such cases of hidden delinquency there are. It frightens me to think about it, and it alarms me because when the same kind of behavior occurs in the slums, those involved are arrested, charged, and started on the road to full-fledged juvenile delinquency.

The publicity given to the Oklahoma City case brought a number of cries of outrage, such as that of the local Council of Churches, which said: "There exists a feeling of guilt on the part of ourselves and the community that we have allowed an atmosphere to develop in which this kind of thing is encouraged."

The council saw in the sex scandal a "pyramiding cultural debauchery" stemming from suggestive movies, television programs, advertisements, books, and magazines.

"This widespread exploitation of sex at the basest and most primitive level of incitement is flooding upon the youth of our community at their times of highest susceptibility to sexual suggestion . . . with neither vocal opposition nor serious protest arising from the community," the council said.

The Reverend Richard Chilton, head of the council's community relations division, added that "this is an omen to us that we must do something." He attributed the outrage to parental permissiveness in moral standards. "We are not concerned enough to get involved," he said, adding that the trouble lies in a combination of incitement to lust and "a lack of moral positiveness in the whole adult society" that has left children without the guidelines they need and want.

Many people of a variety of persuasions became involved in the outcries in Oklahoma City. Dr. Louis J. West, head of the psychiatry department at the University of Oklahoma School of Medicine, was one of them. He urged more and better sex education in school and home and came up with an estimate that "it would cost less to prevent 10,000 rapes a year than to send one person to the moon."

When you sift through all the words, what you really get is the conclusion that a case such as that in Oklahoma City shows an absence of the teaching of moral standards in the home. Norman Vincent Peale has said it much better than I could in his recent book, *Sin, Sex and Self-Control.* The burden of his message is that morality is mainly a matter of self-control; it is much easier to be moral than immoral; but the motivation for morality must come from the home, and it must grow out of the practice of self-control every day, all the time.

A recent case in Ft. Lauderdale, Florida, described in *The New York Times* under the headline "Riddle of Florida Boys: Good Families, High I.Q.'s, 68 Burglaries" illustrates what I am talking about. "At 4 o'clock on a muggy morning eight days ago," *The Times* reported, "a 17-year-old boy dressed entirely in black was arrested near a clump of palm trees in a residential area here. He was carrying a notebook with a razor blade in it. Hanging from a black string around his neck was a curare-dipped needle sealed in an empty bullet shell.

"The youth had an intelligence quotient above 150 and a scholarship to study science at a Swiss university in the fall.

"His arrest touched off an investigation that led authorities several days later to uncover what has since been called the Brain Trust Gang, the Thrush Ring and the Science Fiction Gang.

"Ten boys have been implicated so far, although only three have been charged with any wrongdoing. All have intelligences at the genius level."

The boys had stolen electrical appliances, cameras, radios, stamps, and master keys, according to the police, but most of the loot had been disposed of by three of the boys' mothers, who were *afraid their sons would be caught.* " (Author's italics.) No charges were filed against the mothers.

In groups of two or three, and sometimes alone, the boys had committed at least sixty-eight burglaries and perhaps one hundred. They had stolen chemicals to manufacture bombs, a quantity of dynamite sticks, and ingredients to make nerve gas and the hallucinatory drug LSD, the police said, and were alleged to have concocted schemes for blowing up a bank and using the proceeds to build a laboratory for research to benefit mankind.

According to *The Times,* "the boys had three things in common—superior intelligence, attendance except for one in a nationally known experimental high school and, according to authorities, permissive mothers."

All the boys were from middle-class or wealthy homes. Their parents included a newspaper editor, a building contractor, a high school teacher, a garage owner, a truck driver, a salesman, two secretaries, a clerk, and a retired business-man. The mother of one, when confronted with the sworn confession of her son, shouted at the police: "You beat that out of my boy! He never signed anything like that!" Another mother commented: "If they did these things maybe it was because they were bored. I believe it's more talk than anything else. Kids have a lot of imagination, especially bright ones, and they say a lot of things to impress other kids and even the police, who they think are stupid. It looks to me as if that's what happened here."

What had they done "to impress other kids"? The charges against them included breaking into a home and covering the walls and floors with hot tar and feathers, vandalizing a church, and stealing from a hospital, a school, and a dynamite storage shed.

"We did not have any moral principles," one of the boys later told policemen.

Another said: "We needed recognition. We were the intellectual leaders, but we wanted recognition, we wanted to be accepted by other groups. Of course, when this came out, no one considered any part of it heroic."

And a third told the police: "We began to what you might say rationalize reasons for our activities, that is, almost develop a platform as to why we did things. In doing so, we also cut down on our general trivial operations, as it was considered that they served no useful purpose.

"The criminal activity itself was now rather something to be frowned upon and to be cut down to a minimum. We began to dwell on fantasy. We were getting more kicks out of talking about our exploits than actually doing them."

In case that is not enough, let me add the comment of Dr. Arthur Wolfe, director of Nova High School, the elite institution attended by the boys. He parroted the permissiveness of the parents when he said that the boys had not harmed anyone physically, and added, "I don't think this would have eventually led to more serious crimes because on the one or two occasions when they encountered anybody while committing a crime they fled." He also assured the boys that they would graduate on schedule.

This case is one of the most shocking I have ever heard about, even more so than an incident on Long Island in which permissiveness was carried to an extreme in the vandalism of a mansion. A deputy sheriff took me not long ago on a most unforgettable tour of the wreckage left after a night of "fun" indulged in by children of the privileged class. It was a journey through a nightmare of destruction in a home that had been pillaged and vandalized by teen-agers after a gala debutante party at an estate nearby. The youngsters had driven their sports cars across lawns, uprooting bushes and furrowing the once well-manicured grass. Windows were splintered. Walls were pock-marked and smeared with paint. Lights and plaster had been smashed with sledge hammers. Hatchets had been used to hack away paneling.

Who did all this? Bored, frustrated rich kids with plenty of money in their pockets and every *material* object that their parents could give them. But nowhere along the line, apparently, had anyone instilled in them a feeling for good citizenship, an awareness of their responsibility, or even a sense of neighborliness. The court appearances of the few youngsters who were arrested were a farce. Well-paid lawyers saw to it that the "pranksters" were placed in the custody of their parents with nothing more than a scolding. One father said, "They were only letting off steam." Some steam, I'd say—about $400,000 worth!

Parental delinquency was mixed with permissiveness and shaken well with generous portions of alcohol at the notorious teen-age drinking parties in Darien, Connecticut, in which parents served youngsters liquor in their homes and then let them go out on the highways where two were killed in automobile accidents. A boy involved in one of the accidents later was arrested on a narcotics charge. Several parents were fined in the drinking cases, but no one went to jail. If this had happened in Brooklyn, the Bronx, or Harlem, I am confident that the jail population would have been enlarged.

The permissiveness of many affluent parents is not the only impact wealth has on delinquency. Prosperity itself is a contributory factor. One would think that crime—including juvenile crime—would be more prevalent in bad times than good, but a glance at charts depicting delinquency trends shows just the opposite. I found some pertinent comments about the relationship of delinquency and prosperity recently while reading Roul Tunley's *Kids, Crime and Chaos: A World Report on Juvenile Delinquency.** He recounted a chat he had had with a small-town mayor during a visit to Sicily.

"I wish we had some of that juvenile delinquency you have," the Mayor told Tunley. "We could use it."

"You mean delinquency's a good thing?" Tunley asked.

"Well, I wouldn't say it's exactly a *good thing,*" the Mayor hedged. "But we could use the good things that always go with it—those nice, new factories, the houses, the motor cars. In short, prosperity!"

* Quoted by permission.

Tunley acknowledged surprise at this. He had been hearing for years from "experts" in the United States that it was poverty, slums, and depressed living conditions that caused delinquency.

"You don't believe me," the Mayor said. " . . . But look at it the way I see it. Down south here, we have no money, no industry, no progress. Nobody goes any place because they can't afford it. Besides there are no cars. The family is close; the church is strong. We have crime, of course—vendettas and bandits and robberies—but that's a serious business, far too serious to trust to children. We leave it to the grownups. Consequently, we have little delinquency. Now, up north things are different. Everything's humming. New factories are going up, people are moving to the cities, there's full employment and everybody's buying automobiles and apartments. The result? They've got delinquents all over the place!

". . . Look at your own country. You had a low rate of delinquency in the years of the Depression. Now things are better and you've got a lot more. You're just paying the price of prosperity."

Yes, it *is* ironical, isn't it, that one of the major prices of economic well-being is the criminality of our young people? The Sicilian mayor was right. Delinquency rates did drop during the Depression of the 1930's, and the rise after World War II was broken only by the postwar recession. Mrs. Katherine B. Oettinger, chief of the Children's Bureau, also has concluded that delinquency apparently cannot be traced *directly* to poverty, slums, or even a lack of recreational facilities. It is, she believes, "more likely to increase in a time of prosperity than in a time of depression. This seeming paradox makes us question whether the present high rate of delinquency may be a consequence of the social phenomena of our affluent society, the mobility of our population and the rootlessness it produces, *the deterioration of our sense of values when everything else comes so easily.*"

There are other reasons for blaming prosperity. First, not everyone is prosperous. The "haves" have a lot, while the "have nots" have less than ever, relatively speaking. The family on relief, the low-wage earner, the father with a fixed income, all have to struggle much harder to exist in the inflationary conditions that inevitably accompany prosperity. The struggling father's children see more affluent youngsters driving their own cars or the family's second car, buying hi-fi sets and records, and stocking wardrobes with the latest styles. What do his children do about this? Unfortunately those from homes where moral values have been neglected will go out and steal what they cannot afford to buy. Auto thefts have increased sharply, for example, and when arrested many of the culprits turn out to be kids who just wanted to go out for a joy ride.

In order to see the picture more clearly, I consulted the statistical evidence on juvenile misbehavior, which J. Edgar Hoover recently branded the most appalling aspect of the entire panorama of crime in the United States. The juvenile crime rate is rising out of proportion to the crime rate as a whole and also out of proportion to the increase in the teenage population, according to "Uniform Crime Reports," published by the FBI. As I pointed out earlier, the statistics show that the more economically secure neighborhoods and suburbs are producing more than their share of young troublemakers.

In 1964, for example, arrests of persons between ten and seventeen increased far more than the population of that age group. This rise was accompanied by an intensity in the degree of violence committed. If juvenile infractions proceed at this rate for the next twenty years, we will be in real trouble, particularly if prosperity continues to accelerate as it has in the last few years.

The FBI figures point up the fact that at the heart of the delinquency problem in the United States is the boy between fifteen and seventeen. Sixteen is the peak age, for that is the age at which education is no longer compulsory in most of our states. The youngster without motivation to continue his education is turned loose, so to speak. Of those who get into trouble, about half are involved in serious crimes against property.

Here are some recently gathered specifics about youthful offenders:

• Forcible rape—Nearly two thirds of all individuals arrested for rape in 1964 were under twenty-five, with the highest arrest rate being among the eighteen-to-twenty-one group. *The largest increase in arrests for this offense occurred in prosperous suburbia,* which makes one wonder if it is not in part a matter of more arrests rather than a rise in the actual crimes; in other words, perhaps the delinquency gradually is coming out of hiding.

• Robbery—One out of five solved robbery cases involved persons under eighteen, with the sharpest increase among those under eighteen. Juvenile arrests for robbery in the suburbs were up while those in other areas were down. Youths under twenty-five made up more than two thirds of all who were arrested for robbery.

- Burglary—Eighty per cent of the total arrested were under twenty-five, with the highest rate in the upper teens.
- Auto theft—In the suburbs, auto thefts were up 15 per cent. Offenders under eighteen accounted for nearly two thirds of the arrests; those under twenty-five were responsible for nearly all of the arrests on this charge.
- Narcotics charges—There was a sharp increase in arrests on these charges. Nationally, about half the narcotics arrests in 1964 involved the use of opium derivatives, which include heroin.

In the five years covered by 1960 to 1964, the total number of crimes of violence and against property rose most sharply among young people. The principal increases were for burglary, auto theft, murder, larceny, forcible rape, aggravated assault, and robbery. *The sharpest rises of all crimes reported during the five years were in the suburbs, not urban slums.*

What does all this mean? Mr. Hoover was not content merely to recite figures. He ventured an explanation and offered some suggestions on possible courses of action. To his way of thinking, the best remedy for juvenile delinquency would be the establishment of *real* standards of conduct for young people, supported by *real* authority and a set of rewards for compliance and punishments for violations.

"Parents are the key to this approach," he said. "They must legislate the code, police it, prosecute infractions, pass judgment on the conduct and execute justified punishment or provide earned rewards for their children. Delinquent parents beget delinquent children; good parents rear good children. Of course, there are exceptions, but these are rare and society could easily cope with them. By overcoming and correcting adult delinquency we can greatly reduce the delinquency of children.

"Law-enforcement agencies, teachers, churches and other such individuals and organizations can greatly augment the parents' efforts in setting proper examples and providing needed training for the young of our nation. At best, however, they are poor substitutes for responsible parents. . . . Today's youth need not become victims of the unparalleled freedom and material benefits they enjoy, if only thinking parents will take the time and effort to afford the youngsters a proper perspective and sense of values."

There is scarcely anyone from the halls of Congress to the local PTA and church group who does not agree that juvenile delinquency has become one of our major problems. It touches just about every community and far more homes than is readily realized, taking into account the families that are victimized by the delinquents as well as the families that breed them. At the forefront of efforts to do something about delinquency is the Children's Bureau, which has called for a massive attack on all fronts to counteract "the rapid pace of change of values, family mobility, unprecedented prosperity."

This is a fine statement of lofty intentions. Now we need to find out how this massive attack is to be waged, and by what forces. Where will the schools stand in this battle? And where will the churches be? The major strategy in this offensive should be a war on prosperity. I do not advocate abandoning the much-needed war on poverty, but we should attack those elements of prosperity that are negating so many of the benefits of economic well-being. What we need is a crusade, one that will return parents to the home and make them once more the fountain of moral and ethical values for their children, and one that will bring all of us together in an unrelenting effort to inflate moral standards along with our pocketbooks.

# 5

## The Part-Time Parents

Earlier I mentioned Larry. He made an important contribution to my study of parenthood because he not only had
been the victim of inadequate parents but also had failed at
fatherhood himself. A product of affluent neglect, by the time
Larry became a parent he was such a miserable excuse for a
human being that he simply could not handle responsibility
and therefore was unable to function as either a husband or a
father.

It was on a brisk fall day that one of our workers brought
Larry into our Brooklyn center. "Brought" is not the right
word for it, actually. He was literally dragged in, a filthy,
tattered, trembling mess, half starved and scarcely able to
speak. It took two of our staff members to peel off the rags he
was wearing, bathe him, and get him into the first bed he had
slept in for weeks. Then for two days he went through the
unspeakable tortures of withdrawal from drugs. This is an

ordeal that is sickening to behold. I know of no more practical lesson in the evils of addiction than watching a junkie go through "cold turkey." We have a movie, in almost too vivid color, of one of our boys going through withdrawal and it has proven effective in our prevention program. Youngsters who have seen the film have turned away saying, "No, sir, not for me!" We also show it to our reformed addicts once in a while as a reminder of what they endured and what they face if they return to heroin.

Included in our therapy at Teen Challenge is a requirement that addicts go through cold turkey without medication. If you give them something to relieve the misery, withdrawal becomes too easy for them and they are more likely to pick up the needle again. After cold turkey, they have to shape up or get out. We require every boy and girl at our center to help with the chores, study the Bible, and attend chapel services. Later we give them whatever educational and occupational help they need to get along in society. This usually is done at our rehabilitation centers—for boys a Pennsylvania farm and for girls a country home on a former estate in Garrison, New York. Recently we also launched a "re-entry program," through which we provided housing, counseling and spiritual guidance to young people before sending them back into society. When they have worked in jobs long enough to establish bank accounts and have proved they are really ready to be independent, they are allowed to go out on their own.

All of this is done without charging one penny, regardless of whether an addict has financial resources—and most are destitute. Once in a while the families of the young people we save will make a contribution to help us keep going, but we rely mainly on voluntary gifts from individuals, religious groups, and foundations for our continued existence. Somehow we continue to grow despite the economic pressures upon us.

We never have received one cent from Larry's family, although they are wealthy and his father has written him letters thanking God for what we have done for him. This makes no difference to us. However, it might mean something to Larry. He has come a long way from the gibbering, drooling creature we brought in off the streets. We could not get a coherent story from him for nearly a week. He would just stare at us with glazed blue eyes and mutter. Gradually his story began to come out as he gained strength from rest and good food and began to accept our confidence as we prayed for him and tried to talk to him. Now, a year later, he has been shown a new way of life.

I call Larry a boy, although he is in his twenties, which is beyond the age of most of those we help. But in many ways he had the immaturity of a teen-ager when I first saw him. Whenever we have a chance at the end of a busy day, Larry and I like to sit and talk about his life and his hopes for the future. His experience illustrates much of what I have been saying about why kids go wrong—or right. Parent trouble is too often the answer.

One night I asked him, "Why did you stay with us, Larry?"

"Because I was tired," he replied. "I couldn't help myself any more. I had been using drugs for years. It was costing me $100 a day. I got the money by burglary, stealing, selling narcotics to kids and any other vice I could make money from. It is pretty awful to think about when you realize what I gave up to be a bum."

What had he left behind? A college career and a good job

to follow, a wife, a child, friends, and his own self-respect. I omitted his parents, and soon you will see why.

Larry was born and reared in a Midwestern suburb where his father was an executive of a large manufacturing company. The father had made it the hard way, as one of eight children of an impoverished immigrant. The children had had to leave school and go to work to keep the family going. From the time they were ten years old, all of them had worked, but they always had a mother and father to go home to. Without an adequate education but with ambition and drive that more than made up for it, Larry's father forged ahead and made his place in the world. He, as so many others like him, made the mistake of lavishing material things on his own children. Possessions came to mean love to him, and he wanted his children to have all the possessions he never had when he was a child. The trouble was that he did not give them time as well.

The family lived in a rambling English Tudor-style home with a three-car garage, cook, housekeeper, and gardener. Each member of the household had his own room with connecting bath. Larry had the run of a well-stocked library— and a well-stocked bar when nobody was looking. The basement recreation room was equipped with table tennis and pool tables and all sorts of games.

This does not sound anything like the crowded tenements that some of our other boys came from, but there was one distressing similarity in the family's life, and that did not lie in the material things at all. Larry was neglected, just as much as some of the underprivileged youngsters who come to us from homes without fathers or mothers or where one parent is living out of wedlock with one person after another. What happened to Larry because of parental neglect was no different from what had happened to Bobby Foster. Larry, however, was still alive, through no fault of his own, while Bobby was dead.

"We had a nice home and everything we wanted that money could buy," Larry told me. "But my father was always away on business and my mother would run off to Florida any time she could find an excuse for the trip. My brother and sister were just about grown when I arrived. I came to my parents rather late in life. They did not want me when I was born and later did not want to be bothered with me.

"I was raised by a housekeeper, when I was at home. They kept me out of the way most of the time. I went to boarding school every fall and then shortly after school was out in June, I was sent to camp. I was lucky if I saw my parents thirty days a year. I've had part-time parents all my life."

Without having any real understanding of what was going on, Larry resented the lack of attention when he was a child. Disappointment after disappointment led him to do what many neglected children do to try to get their parents interested in them. He rebelled.

"First I got into little scrapes, little fights, little childish things," he said, "because my parents weren't there when I needed them. Sometimes I got into trouble in school or had some difficulty with my studies. I had only the housekeeper to go to, but I didn't want to bother her. I would write to my parents wherever they were but tell them only the good things. The letters we exchanged always ended with the word 'love' but it was just on paper.

"I knew how to drive, so I began sneaking my father's Cadillac out for joy rides. I would get a couple of friends and we'd push the car out of the garage and down the driveway so nobody could hear us, and then we'd roar off and have a wonderful time. I never stole cars in the sense of really stealing them, but I guess this *was* stealing in a way. I was a thirteen-year-old punk in dungarees and a T-shirt, but I was a big shot to my friends when I was behind the wheel of a high-powered car."

This went on for a long time without any difficulty. Then one night the police stopped the boys for speeding, and they were in deep trouble. An officer discovered they had been puffing on marijuana cigarettes.

When Larry's father appeared with an expensive lawyer at the jail, he arranged for the boy to be released and packed him off to a camp on the promise that "they'll put some sense into him." His father could not afford the risk of keeping him at home where he might get into more trouble, which would have spoiled a budding political career. It also might have upset Larry's mother.

"I can't be sure what would have happened if my father had kept me at home," Larry says now, "but I have a feeling that if he had put his arm around my shoulder and said a few kind words and spent some time with me that summer, my life might have been different."

As it was, the rebellion continued. Larry got a girl "in trouble," but his father managed to keep that quiet by paying the bills and giving the girl a substantial sum of money. All she had to do was sign a few papers. Then Larry started drinking heavily. Finally came an addiction to marijuana, then heroin.

Larry has explained what happened this way: "I gave up on myself long before I gave up on my parents. When you give up on yourself, you're lost and you can't find yourself. I couldn't find God either, even though I had been given a religious upbringing. My parents sent me to Sunday school, but they never went to church themselves. Finally I figured as long as they didn't care about religion enough to go to church, why should I? I stopped going. It was as simple as that.

"I was lucky in one way, I guess, however. I was unusually bright and a quick study in school. I would have graduated from college if my luck had held out. I did manage to get through three years of college and had it pretty easy. There always was plenty of money for dates and things and I had my own car and no parents to supervise me. That was the whole trouble. I might have done better with no car and a job and parents who asked me how I was doing once in a while. My father's only concern was that I should get through college and then he would see that I got a good job. I think now it is better to work for things.

"I started using drugs as part of my rebellion, not to experiment or anything like that. I was going to get even with my parents. I was going to show them! I was going to get their attention. It didn't work, and a lot of people have suffered as a result."

Narcotics were the reason Larry did not finish college. He was expelled from school when the dean found him in a men's room with a hypodermic syringe. "It got in the papers and embarrassed my father," Larry said. "He asked me to leave town, and I did. I haven't seen him since."

Like so many other lost and bewildered young people, Larry went to New York. With three years of college behind him, he found a job in a downtown Manhattan office and seemed to be getting along all right on his own. He married one of the stenographers in the office typing pool and they had a baby, an event recognized by his father with a handsome check—not a visit, but a check. Larry and his wife devoted many evenings to discussions of how they would spend the money, meanwhile putting it to work in a savings account. He thought a lot about that money. It got to the point where it occupied most of his waking moments until one day, without telling his wife, he played hookey from the office, took all the money out of the bank, and headed for Yonkers Raceway where he lost every cent in a week.

Unable to tell his wife the truth and lacking the courage even to face her after work each night, Larry began dropping into the neighborhood bar for a few drinks before going home. Then he stopped going home at all. He permanently "forgot" to go to work. A narcotics pusher found him one night, and that finished Larry's efforts to establish a good life.

I could write the rest of the story of Larry's downfall with my eyes closed, I have heard it so many times from so many addicts. First he sniffed heroin powder. Then he skin-popped; that means he inserted small portions of the powdered narcotics under his skin. Finally, he mainlined, which means he jabbed it right into his bloodstream. He was hooked.

A life of crime to support the habit followed. He was arrested eight times. Once, the authorities sent him to a municipal hospital for a "cure." Then he was sent to the Federal Hospital at Lexington, Kentucky, where drug addicts are treated but seldom cured. The other arrests landed him in jail.

While Larry was at Lexington, his wife decided to divorce him. She had tried and tried to help him, but without success. So she left town, got the divorce, and later married a rising young attorney who has adopted the boy Larry was not man enough to care for. The boy is just starting school now. From what Larry hears from his ex-wife and his father, the youngster is one of the nicest kids in his block and has a good relationship with his adopted father. He does not know much about Larry, who would like to see him some time but feels now that it would be better to leave the boy alone.

"I'll have to start my life over, now that I've decided not to be a rebel any more," he said not long ago. "I know now that I was not rebelling against my parents, but really more against myself. I could not have liked myself very much or I would never have done the things I did."

He has an idea that he let off steam when he was a teen-ager not only in an effort to communicate his need for love and attention but also to demand discipline that he never did receive. "To me, there is more to discipline than spanking a child or bawling him out," he explained to a class of newly reformed addicts one day. "Every time I got into trouble in the early years of my rebellion, my parents would condone it. They'd say, 'He's just letting off a little steam.' I think parents should show their love for children by holding a strong hand over them so they don't go astray or become wild. They should watch a youngster's associates. I know my parents didn't even know or care whom I was with, and this is how I started on narcotics."

Only now does Larry feel that he is beginning to get any discipline from his father. He read me part of a letter he had received from his father after he had written to tell the family about Teen Challenge and what it was doing for him and others.

"Received your letter and am happy to hear that you are getting along," the father wrote. "I hope this is finally 'it.' "

Larry paused a moment and looked at me. "It took him all these years to learn to care," he said.

The rest of the letter reported on the health and activities of other members of the family. His mother was "just fine, gone to Florida for a few weeks," and his sister had undergone a serious operation. His father had a new car that he could not drive because of a heart condition, so he hired a chauffeur. And then he said he was praying for Larry.

"Drop me a line," the father added. "Don't violate any rules, and try to fight this battle to win or it will be lost for you."

I smiled at Larry and said, "That certainly is the letter of a father who cares. And he is praying for you. That is important."

Larry confirmed this. "It's the first time he's ever written like this in all the years we have been corresponding. He made me feel good because he did not just scribble a note asking where to send me money. He was sending love, too, this time.

"I guess in a sense he was bawling me out, too, between the lines. That's just fine with me. And he is also showing a little pride for the first time, and that makes me feel good, too, because I know there is love there behind it all. It's been a long time since I felt this was so."

I am rewarded for my work with Teen Challenge by talks such as this one with Larry. It could become discouraging at times if it were not for those with whom we succeed so well. Work with narcotics addicts has been our main job and continues to be, and our activities in neighborhoods such as the one that bred Larry may lead eventually to establishment of suburban branches of Teen Challenge.

Come with me now on a visit to one of these areas. Let me tell you more about narcotics addiction. What can parents do to help prevent it?

# 6

# "Like Father, Like Son"

In a two-story Georgian brick home on a three-acre plot in a Midwestern suburb, it is a few minutes after midnight. Mrs. S——, having just completed her nightly argument with her husband, is taking her usual potion of two pink and blue sleeping pills. Mr. S—— has polished off his fifth Scotch and soda since dinner. They are just about anesthetized for sleep when the persistent jangle of the telephone jolts them into sufficient consciousness to answer it. Mr. S—— picks up the receiver.

"Is this the S—— residence?"

"Yes."

"This is the police, Sergeant Boggs. We have your boy down here. He's under arrest. Narcotics charge."

The father sobers suddenly.

"But this is impossible! He's right here, at home in bed! At least I *think* he is. Are you sure he is Richard S—— of 22 Pinenut Place?"

Sergeant Boggs was sure. The arraignment was to be in the morning. He was very sorry he could not talk longer because he had several other parents to telephone before dawn. He also called our nearest Teen Challenge Center to see if I was in town. I had asked him to let me know the next time they picked up any juveniles on narcotics charges so I could talk to some of these kids and perhaps their parents, too. By chance I was there. I had spoken at a youth rally earlier in the evening and had decided to stay over and catch a morning plane back to New York.

Hurriedly I dressed and one of our workers drove me to the suburban police station where I found that Richard S—— was one of a dozen or so teen-aged boys and girls who had been picked up in a raid on the unoccupied servants' quarters over the garage on the estate of one of his friends. They were "snorting" heroin, sniffing it through their nostrils, as they had done every Friday night for the last month, when the police barged in. Sniffing "H" had given them some real kicks; they never knew life could be so rosy until . . .

Until a disgruntled girl, who had been derided as a prude and square by the crowd when she turned "chicken" and shunned narcotics, had told her parents about what was going on above the garage and they had gone to the police.

By morning, the news was all over town. This was one story that even rich parents couldn't keep out of the papers. The local newspaper was filled with items about the arrests of the children of some of the community's wealthiest and most prominent citizens on "dope" charges. The local radio and television stations had a field day tracking down distraught parents to ask them for comments. The community was shaken. While people had read about juvenile delinquency and narcotics traffic in big cities, in slums and even in other affluent neighborhoods, they had assumed that "it could never happen here." That kind of thing happens only to underprivileged kids, children of broken homes, minority groups, and youths in *other* places, not in good old Respectableville. Now it had hit this place and no one could, or would, believe it— at first.

The truth sank in gradually and painfully. It not only could but *did* happen here. Lawyers retained by the families of the culprits appeared in court, arranged for the youngsters to be released in bail, and ultimately won suspended sentences for them. During the ordeal, Mrs. S—— confessed that she had found it necessary to step up her nightly potion of barbiturates in order to sleep and her husband had started gulping his liquid tranquilizer straight from the bottle. All the while, young Richard received scoldings at regular intervals and lectures for having allowed himself to become involved in a scandal from which the *family* might never recover.

Nobody thought of sitting down and talking frankly and fairly to Richard in an attempt to find out how he had happened to get into trouble or to educate his by now disturbed conscience. No, his mother and father were so concerned with what had happened to *them* that they failed to consider Richard's tragedy. Not once did they ask themselves, Where did we go wrong? What did we do to contribute to this? They did manage to change the theme of their nightly quarrel slightly to include accusations aimed at one another as to which might have been to blame for Richard's "trouble," but they had no insight into what their real roles in his yielding to temptation might have been.

If Richard is lucky, we at Teen Challenge can establish rapport with him and perhaps help him find himself and build a decent, meaningful life. Or perhaps some other pastoral counselor can help him. We advised the young people we talked to in that community to go to see their ministers, priests, and rabbis and to try to work out their problems with them.

Unfortunately, however, as earlier chapters have made apparent, too many of the youngsters who experiment with narcotics do not get the kind of help they need and must have—or they get it too late. If their parents would only put aside their pill boxes and whisky bottles, they might be able to set the examples that are needed so sorely by youngsters such as Richard, or at the very least provide them with an anchor at home. *Home is where the moral values are* and no courtroom or minister's study will ever replace it.

If you only knew how often remorseful parents have wept in my office over the downfall of their children. If you could hear them say, "How could he have done it?" about a boy almost dead from an overdose of heroin or, "We never suspected for a moment," about a daughter on the verge of giving birth to a child whose father's identity is a question mark. They just can't believe *they* ever made a mistake or a misjudgment, and when you try to suggest that either might be the case, you provoke either stony stares or strings of epithets.

Narcotics addiction is far from limited to teen-agers, of course, and its causes are complex and varied. It is probable that most of the people involved in this deadly game of seeking escape from life are adults. However, more and more youngsters are being victimized by one another and by the cynical narcotics peddler, for whom there is no punishment severe enough. Increasing numbers of teen-agers now experience their first "sniff" of heroin in a school washroom and, once hooked, manage to purchase supplies from student user-pushers or from junkies who peddle it near school grounds.

It is difficult to pinpoint the blame for narcotics addiction, which now is the subject of widespread concern and speculation. If it were possible to isolate the precise causes, the prevention and cure would be relatively simple, but it is like cancer—its origin is really undetermined. This was emphasized when President Kennedy convened a conference of more than four hundred experts at the White House in 1962 to discuss drug abuse. "I don't think there is any field about which there is so much divided opinion, so much possible to do and in some places, limited action," he declared. "This national problem merits national concern."

And there is no moral subject closer to the family than drug addiction. When you consider the thirteen billion potentially lethal doses of barbiturates (sleeping pills), amphetamines (pep pills), and tranquilizers taken in our country every year—at least half of them distributed through illegal channels at prices ranging up to a dollar a pill—and when you consider the thousands of people, many of them teen-agers, who smoke "pot" (marijuana), sniff glue, and use heroin, morphine, or cocaine, you have to accept the fact that the drug and narcotics problem is larger and involves more lives than any of us could possibly comprehend. Entire families suffer from the presence of the addict, who steals from his parents or pawns family treasures to buy "just one more shot," or who causes anguish with his sloth and his own suffering when he is in desperate need of a fix. Strangers, too, are victimized by burglaries, thefts, and assaults by addicts frantic for money to finance the next "deck" of heroin. In short, all of society pays the penalty.

Five members of the Hell Burners Gang introduced me to the sordidness of the narcotics problem. I met them one night several years ago on a tenement stoop in Brooklyn, totally unaware that they were all mainlining heroin addicts although I had been working with them for weeks.

On that sultry summer night, I began preaching the Gospel to them. Promptly they all dozed off. In exasperation, I shook one of the boys and asked him why he was being so rude. "Davie," he said, "can't you see we're goofing? One of our boys went to cop a deck of junk and we're going upstairs for a tea party. You can come up and watch us drill if you want." Soon they were all awake and talking about horse, shit, junk, spike, the man, the bull, dynamite, tea party. I knew I was in another world.

Most of what I had known up until that moment about narcotics was what I had heard from my father's pulpit when visiting ministers and missionaries from far-off places related stories about the opium dens in China. But this was New York City and these were teen-age American boys. They had become my friends, I thought, and had stopped waging gang warfare in the streets. All of them were working "angles," however, to support their narcotics habits.

A boy who did not know me shambled up and immediately suspected I was a narcotics agent posing as a minister, as they often do. I quoted enough Scripture to convince him that I was not a cop and in a few moments I found myself walking with the gang up nine flights of stairs to the roof. On the way, a boy named Shorty plucked a dirty pop bottle from a trash can, filled it with cold water in a community lavatory and struggled panting to the roof obviously in urgent need of a fix. From a pocket he pulled out what he told me were "the works," which included a bottle cap and a hypodermic needle and syringe. One of the boys handed Shorty a deck of heroin, which is a tiny cellophane bag containing just enough of the white powder to cover a thumbnail and costing five dollars.

Shorty removed his belt and pulled it tight around his arm. Then he put the heroin powder into the bottle cap with a few drops of water, lit a match under it and "cooked" it. When it was bubbling, he removed the liquid with an eye dropper and put it into the hypodermic syringe. Quickly he found a vein and injected heroin into his arm. A smile swept his face. He sighed and sank down, leaning against a chimney.

One of the other boys seized the needle. "Don't use it all," he whined. "Save some for me." He and two other boys gave themselves shots from that same dirty needle. The sight made me pass out cold.

The next thing I knew, I was lying on the roof.

"Hey, preacher, are you chicken?" one of them asked.

"Why in the world don't you find a cure?" I urged.

They laughed at me. "Where have you been, preacher?" one of the boys said. "We've been to hospitals, we've been to clinics, we've been to doctors, we've seen head shrinkers, we've been hypnotized." Another interrupted to tell me, "I even went up to a cop and kicked him in the pants so I could get locked up and go through cold turkey and kick the habit."

I assured the boys that I was no sissy, that I could stand seeing blood and other unpleasant sights, but that watching them use that dirty needle for that evil purpose was too much for me. Then I left, having taken the first step toward learning that there is no physical cure known to medical science for narcotics addiction. As I departed, one of the boys clutched my sleeve, looked straight into my eyes and said, "Reverend, there are only three ways out—either O.D. (overdose), suicide, or God."

This was the message I took with me. I knew God. I knew that He had the power. I had the will to try to put that power to work. Teen Challenge's work with narcotics addicts thus was born on a Brooklyn rooftop that July evening. My concern with narcotics since then has been the young addict, and he is our concern in this discussion of parental shortcomings. I tend to blame parents for most of the difficulties their young people get into, but as I have said, no one has the complete answer to the question, "Why do young people become addicted?" No isolated case can be explained by a single situation or set of circumstances. The background leading to addiction usually is so complicated that the addict himself cannot provide a clear or complete history of his own case. However, several basic factors have become evident in most of the cases I have seen, and they are presented in what I consider to be the order of their importance.

1. *Curiosity*. There is inherent in all of us, particularly young people, a spirit of inquiry that inspires experiment and adventure. Many of the addicts we have dealt with at Teen Challenge had been "playing around" with drugs solely out of curiosity. They wanted to find out what all the publicity was about, and they wanted to know "what it feels like" to be high on heroin, first by taking a snort, then by skin-popping. Naturally no young person who has thus experimented had any idea of becoming addicted to this derivative of the opium

poppy, just as surely as no one takes a drink of liquor with the intention of becoming a drunkard. But all the potential addict needs is an introduction to the effect of drugs and he soon will be mainlining the "stuff" directly into his bloodstream and turning his veins into dead black tattoos he will carry the rest of his life. He is hooked, and kicking the heroin habit is far more difficult than learning to say no to an offer of "just one more" drink of whisky.

A large percentage of the addicts treated at our Teen Challenge Centers started on heroin mainly out of curiosity. They were bored and intrigued by the effect the narcotic had on their friends. I have heard the initial experience described as giving a boy the same forbidding feeling one has when walking into a so-called haunted house at midnight.

2. *Ignorance.* Young people who burn the midnight oil to cram for school examinations or try to keep awake at the wheel of a car on a long week-end skiing trip often take benzedrine, amphetamine, or other pep pills or capsules that fend off sleep. They not only stay awake but become so stimulated that when the time for sleep comes they cannot close their eyes. This leads to a sedative. Before they know what has happened, they become addicted to pills. All of this occurs without any prior knowledge of the dangers or realization of what is happening to them.

Many young people become aware of the dangers of being hooked only after they have developed a dependence on drugs. Now they start looking for new and bigger thrills so they can continue feeling the sense of satisfaction that comes with being "high" on narcotics. It is at this point that they move into the deadly progression, from marijuana to morphine to heroin, or from morphine to cocaine to heroin, without really knowing what they are doing except that they are getting some great new kicks out of life.

Lawmakers are beginning to awaken to the fact that all kinds of pills are too easily available to those who should not have them. Laws governing the issuance of prescriptions for all drugs have been lax. The legislatures are trying now to strengthen the regulation of the writing and renewal of prescriptions so that the supplies will be more difficult to obtain.

Parents who take pills often fail to pierce the veil of ignorance surrounding addiction. Those who keep medicine cabinets well stocked with pills and swallow them in front of their children are to blame for the practice of many teen-agers who take their own brand of pills and then wave off criticism with a flippant remark such as "The old man [or the old lady] takes 'em. *They* don't die. *They* never take an O.D. I'm O.K.!"

3. *Acceptance.* People with neurotic tendencies—feelings of inadequacy, insecurity, or rejection—are more susceptible than others to involvement with narcotics. The use of drugs usually starts in group relationships. Teen-agers, for example, will gather in a secluded spot, such as a school basement, an abandoned tenement, a vacant lot, or a home from which parents are habitually absent. Sometimes they start with drinking parties at which a member of the group will introduce "pot," or marijuana cigarettes. Others may bring bottles of cough syrup spiked with codeine or tubes of airplane glue to sniff. Those desiring a mild uplift sip nutmeg dissolved in hot water or milk. Anyone declining to partake of whatever forbidden fruit is offered is branded chicken, so he must go along with the crowd in order to belong. The same dare that starts a youngster on marijuana will lure him into a trial shot

of heroin a few weeks later. Then he is in real trouble. By the time such youngsters stagger to the doorstep of Teen Challenge, often only days from death, pleading for help, they are ready to confess, "If I had only known what I was getting into, I never would have taken the first step." In all likelihood no one, least of all their parents, had discussed the matter with them.

After becoming addicted to win acceptance by the "go-go" crowd, the youngster who finds himself with a monkey on his back suddenly is alone. Narcotics are expensive and now it is every man for himself. Every addict is lonely, a law unto himself, catering only to his obsessive need for a fix. It is ironic and tragic that most teen-agers who get hooked through a need for acceptance in turn seek out others to drag down with them. The most dangerous power of addiction is the power of persuasion it creates in a teen-ager who has "gone the route" and can now capitalize on a need for acceptance he no longer has. We have learned, for example, that an average of twenty-five youngsters are lured into addiction by every teen-age heroin user!

4. *Escape.* Emotionally immature individuals are particularly prone to seek escape from the realities of life. Rather than learn to face difficulties, they seek release through drinking, smoking, or narcotics. Symptoms of their immaturity include unfounded fears, obsessions, and anxieties; feelings of inadequacy, inferiority, and guilt; physical weaknesses, handicaps, and twitching muscles. Persons suffering from any or all of these symptons are likely to feel they are misfits wherever they are. Narcotics offer them escape from facing the true issues of life and accepting its responsibilities, and also make them feel on top of the world for a short time.

I know for a fact that many of the addicts under our care started using narcotics to escape dreadful living conditions and hopeless environmental problems. One addict summed it up for me this way: "I live in a hell and I'm doomed to live in it for life. The only heaven I get comes in a needle and it costs $5 a trip there and back. So let me have my heaven now. Don't lock the gates of heaven on me. I'd rather die. Everybody needs a little heaven."

A sixteen-year-old addict confessed to me, "David, Mom and Dad told me I'd never make it because I was always fighting with my sister and with the kids in school. I failed three grades and they put me in a special school. Teachers tell me I'm a failure. Nobody likes me and it gets worse all the time. When I take a fix I feel like I'm a success. I don't care then how my family feels. I don't even hate the teacher. But I feel like hell when I'm not high."

5. *Exploitation.* To minimize his own guilt over being enslaved to narcotics, a youngster may persuade or even force others to join in the "fun." An adolescent tends to yield easily to the pressure of companions who have already been experimenting with liquor or drugs. In rare instances, pure selfishness motivates an addict to exploit his friends. In order to insure a steady supply of drugs for himself, he seeks customers among friends to whom he can sell narcotics. He also finds that when his own supply of narcotics runs out, he can borrow from his addicted friends.

6. *Victimization.* A tragic number of young people are trapped into taking drugs by vicious underworld characters or older companions who persuade them to take one "sample" fix, just one, "to see what it is like," and then either dominate them with threats of exposure if they do not become regular

customers or promise greater thrills to come. Drug pushers take advantage of youthful ignorance and the desire to experiment to turn children into addicts, and sometimes even to thieves and murderers as well.

With these six factors in mind, let us look at some of the specific answers given by the youngsters themselves when asked why they have turned to drugs.

"It seemed that everybody was doing it, so I decided to try it, too. At first I didn't like it, but now I do."

"I started sniffing heroin with friends at a dance. Most of the kids I knew were using it, so why shouldn't I? Even my girl uses it now."

"Most of the guys in my neighborhood were messing around with heroin."

"My boy friend started me on the needle. He said if I really loved him I'd try it. Now I'm hooked."

"Why not buy it? You can get pills on any corner in my neighborhood and it costs only fifty cents a fix."

"I just tagged along after the gang until I got caught stealing money to buy drugs and was sent to jail."

"After my mother and father broke up, I just didn't care what happened any more. Heroin made me forget my troubles."

"My girl friend broke off with me and I started taking heroin to get even with her."

"My father was my only real friend and when he died I lost myself in heroin to get even with the world."

"Heroin makes me feel like I can do anything I want. It makes me feel smarter than everyone else."

Had enough? This is a fair sample of responses. They dramatize the absence of adult supervision of young people's activities. They dramatize a lack of moral or religious values in the lives of many. They also dramatize the fact that it is unmercifully easy to obtain narcotics. But, hopefully, there are some preventive measures parents can take.

# 7

## Danger Ahead. Watch the Signs

What do you say to a minister who falls on his knees before you and cries for help for his two teen-age sons who have become drug addicts? I faced this dilemma when the man, broken by the tragedy, came to my office. He had just resigned the pulpit he had filled for twenty-seven years and he did not know where else to turn. He came to Teen Challenge. With him were two handsome boys, seventeen and eighteen years old, who slouched in chairs beside my desk and smirked while their father wept.

The clergyman had learned only the day before that his sons had been charged with the use and possession of narcotics. Between sobs, he told me the story, a story made all the more tragic because he had become something of an "expert" on addiction. He had read everything he could find on problems of delinquency and addiction and had passed the information on to his congregation in his Sunday sermons. He had counseled parents whose children were addicts. He had accompanied children to court and had visited them and prayed over them at the Federal Narcotics Hospital in Lexington, Kentucky. And he also recalled the many times that he had gone to the police to report thefts from his own home in the erroneous belief that burglars had broken in.

Now here he was, chagrined, stricken, and remorseful at having been so naïve, so belatedly aware that he had been out of touch with his boys—so out of touch that he had not even suspected that it was they who had been stealing from him and pawning the loot to support their heroin habits. True, he had noticed that they had been losing weight, oversleeping, skipping school, and occasionally had bloody marks on their arms. He had been mildly annoyed when they scratched their noses, pulled their ears, and appeared otherwise restless as they ate dinner with the rest of the family.

All these are marks of the addict. He knew that. But how could he associate the symptoms with his own children? When the police called to say they had arrested his sons on narcotics charges, his first reaction was one of disbelief, but then he began remembering things, and finally he realized the charges were true. He went to the boys and arranged for them to leave jail on bail pending trial, and for the first time in many months he sat down and talked with them, begging their forgiveness for having spent so much time with the children of his congregation and so little with them.

Now that they had been caught, the boys told their father the whole story. They had been running with a group of teenagers who were experimenting with narcotics, and decided to try it themselves "just for kicks." First they sniffed, and they liked it. That marked the beginning of three years of "taking the route"; within a year, they were mainlining heroin into their veins at a cost of $25 to $40 a day. To support this kind of habit, they had to rob and steal. Their own father was one of their victims.

Upon learning the terrible truth, the father was so embarrassed and hurt that he immediately resigned from his church and vowed that he would not preach again until he had found help for his own children. It was then that he heard about our Teen Challenge program and brought the boys to us.

I was deeply moved by the father's anguish. As he sat opposite me pouring out his heart, the boys—apparently unmoved—just sat there staring into space. I turned to the older boy, George, and asked him to remove his hat, in respect for his father. It took him quite a while to comply. Then he fidgeted about as though he was thinking of leaving the room. At my request, the father rose and went outside so I could speak privately to the boys. I thought I might be able to reach them, but only a few minutes with them made it clear that neither wanted help, that they had lost all respect for their father, that they were not ready to join any program that would take them away from the "Big H."

"I love the stuff," George said, "and I'm going to keep it up in spite of everybody."

"Yeah," was all the other boy could manage to say.

I called the father back and told him that we could help people only if they wanted to be helped and that clearly his sons were not yet that desperate. The father shook my hand and was still weeping and shaking his head when he left. At his side were his two mocking sons, snickering as if to say, "The poor old man just doesn't understand."

This father gave me a lot to think about. Here was a so-called expert preaching about addiction to his church members and yet so blind when it came to his own sons that at home he had not been able to put together all the evidence that spells addiction. I decided that if this father, with all that he knew about it, had failed to detect addiction in his sons, I should try to spell out clearly and unmistakably some warning signals, and, more important, urge parents to be ever alert for them. I hope I can help prevent similar episodes in other families by pinpointing the scores of telltale symptoms we have observed at Teen Challenge among the addicts we have helped. Parents should ask themselves, Do any of these appear in my children? And if any of them do, they should act immediately; the earlier addiction is detected, the easier it is to cure.

The signs of addiction are easy to spot if one is really looking for them. Generally speaking, persons addicted to narcotics display the following symptoms:

- Needle marks on arms or legs.
- Watery eyes.
- Furtive glances.
- Chronic drowsiness.
- Marked restlessness with body spasms and a tendency to walk fast.
- Easily upset stomach.
- Ulcerous sores on arms, legs, and body.
- Uncontrollable giddiness.
- A strong body odor.
- Habitual scratching or rubbing of nose.
- Lack of sex drive.
- Frequent dizziness.
- Obvious mental and physical deterioration.
- Periodic states of either preoccupation or talkativeness.

- Depression and despondency.
- Persecution complex.

A youngster who is addicted is sleepy most of the time. He loses interest in school and cannot concentrate on his studies. He has no interest in athletics or in any other form of exercise. He is irritable, tells stupid lies, or refuses to talk at all because of his preoccupation with himself. He may develop boils or abcesses at the point of his injections due to the use of unsanitary equipment.

Lewis, one of the former addicts I told about earlier, regrets that his parents didn't keep a closer watch over him. "I'd check," he says, "how long a kid stays in the bathroom. If he is there very long, he might be taking drugs. I used to do that. I have told my mother to watch my kid brothers, to search their clothes when they came home at night and make sure they come home right after school.

"It's a good idea to look for some of the signs of narcotics. If arms or handkerchiefs have any blood on them, it might mean a kid has been using the needle. Also, when a kid gets into the habit of wearing sunglasses all the time, it's a sign he might be using drugs. When he gets high his eyes get very red, especially from marijuana, and his pupils get very small. People can tell from looking at you if you have been smoking pot. The dark glasses help, too, because when a fellow is high on marijuana, he can't stand the sun."

All the signs I have mentioned are bad enough, but eventually a parent may get the fright of his life when his child starts going through the hell of cold turkey. When an addict cannot get the narcotics he craves or the medication to make withdrawal easier, he becomes first uneasy, then restless and irritable. His eyes water as though he had hay fever; he yawns and his nose begins to run and itch. His muscles twitch violently and pangs of pain shoot up and down his back, arms, and legs. Violent cramps stab him in the stomach. He vomits and has diarrhea and involuntarily kicks his legs and jerks his arms. He curls up like a puppy in bed or on the floor and shivers under all the coverings he can find, even in summer. His feet are constantly atwitch. Whatever sleep he gets is sporadic at first; then he is totally unable to close his eyes. Because he cannot retain food or liquid, he may lose as much as ten pounds in twenty-four hours. On the third day, he is in the depths of his own private hell. This is cold turkey and the ordeal by which we at Teen Challenge make our first strides toward breaking an addict of his habit. If an addict is not willing to go through cold turkey, we feel he cannot find a cure and salvation.

Now you may ask, "But where do youngsters get the narcotics that put them in such a state? Can't we stamp out their sources of supply or at least keep them away from such places?" These questions are revealing, for you will ask them only if you are a parent who has not up to now given your children the kind of discipline that will keep them out of undesirable environments. Such a parent might try looking where the police have learned to look, which is just about any place teen-agers congregate and where suspicious-looking people seem to seek out youngsters. The places and people to watch out for are:

• Corner hangouts that attract older boys and girls.

• Rooming houses and apartment buildings where there is an unusual flow of people in and out.

• A person loitering on the street who seems to be having dealings with others.

- Outside junior and senior high schools where older boys and men loiter.
- Teen-agers smoking in groups, on corners, in basements or in hallways. If the smoke they exhale has an odd aroma, it is likely to be marijuana.
- Well-dressed, "sharp" looking individuals who just hang around candy stores and luncheonettes and have no apparent legitimate means of income.

Special attention should be given also to roofs, cellars, stairways, halls, and vacant buildings where people are known to congregate. Such places are known to addicts as "shooting galleries." Evidence found in them would be such items as the empty gelatin capsules or small cellophane squares of paper in which narcotics are peddled; medicine droppers; bent safety pins; burned matches; bent spoons or bottle caps; and pieces of cotton. The spoons and bottle caps are used for "cooking" the heroin over lighted matches; the injection is made with the scratch of a safety pin into a vein. Hypodermic needles come later and are seldom left behind.

Once you find the sources of supply and the places of use, what do you do? I should ask, What *should* you do? You can go to the police. You can confront your child with the evidence and ask him if he needs help. Above all, you can show him you love him and want to help him. Recriminations will only drive him deeper into his misery. But be assured, *he will want to get out,* and badly, even if he won't admit it.

I am sorry to say, however, that there is no certain solution to addiction. Answers to this phase of the narcotics problem are hard to come by. We live in an age in which everything seems to be getting more complicated and specialized: Science, medicine, economics—everything—is growing so intricate that it is increasingly difficult for ordinary people even to begin to understand them. The specific problem of drug addiction is equally complex. Governor Nelson A. Rockefeller of New York summarized the difficulty this way: "Obviously, something should be done about drug addiction. The question is 'what?' As we all know, drug addiction is a problem which has many sides. There are those who say that the penal laws should be made even stiffer than they are. On the other hand, there are those who say this is primarily a medical problem and stiffer penal laws only aggravate the difficulty.

"It seems to me that there is one course of action upon which there can be no disagreement. That is the need for research. If somebody tells me that there is no established cure for heroin addiction in this age of medical miracles, my response is that we must redouble our efforts to find one. The emphasis must be on research. Because there is no established cure for the type of addiction which represents 87 per cent of the problem, everything else that we do is at best a temporary palliative and does not go to the core of the problem. Even in so complicated a problem as narcotics addiction, however, the personal touch which comes from private philanthropy and human charity remains essential."

As important as research may be, that is not the real avenue to relief. I believe corrective measures must be taken. We must reach the potential addict—you might call him the pre-addict —before he becomes addicted. It has been said that if the living conditions of many of our addicts had been improved, they could have been saved. But you may ask, Why do we have so many addicts living in beautiful homes and with unlimited allowances? To the eye, their homes may seem perfect, but underneath, as we saw in Larry's case, lie moral and spiritual conditions that, if corrected, could spare children much tragedy.

We also need more than education, which often is offered as a solution. True, education is an important and valuable tool but it simply is not enough. Consider the number of doctors, nurses, and laboratory technicians who have become addicts. They not only are educated but are educated in the dangers of narcotics. There is a weak spot in every suggested panacea for drug addiction, except one—the exception is a vitalizing spiritual experience that will give a young person the wish, the will, and the power to say No, to resist. Only God can provide that power. And it must be generated in the home and the church.

The most effective weapon in keeping a young person from being addicted is the security of a well-adjusted, rewarding home life, with family ties made strong by love. The youth must have the confidence of his entire family, and they must have his confidence. A lack of mutual confidence between parent and offspring sends many a young person into the streets; and it is only this confidence that will save him after he has toppled into the gutter.

Once a young person has become involved with narcotics, he can be rescued only if he will accept help. It is impossible to break the habit without cooperative, sympathetic, gentle assistance. Just as Alcoholics Anonymous draws its success from one person helping another, so cures for narcotics addiction are dependent on the brotherhood of personal assistance. This is what we give youngsters who come to Teen Challenge. We offer prayers and spiritual guidance, shelter and medical treatment when necessary, but we also assign to each addict at least one of our workers, who stays at his side night and day throughout the cold turkey ordeal.

This is one kind of cure; there are others. The final answer will lie in prevention, for as with any disease, it is better to prevent than to cure. Our experience at Teen Challenge has led us to conclude that the following are the most important preventive steps that can be taken in the home.

1. A youngster must be encouraged to have a positive goal in life. It behooves parents to develop in their children an intelligent appreciation of the dignity of labor so that they can prepare to earn an honest living. Youngsters should be taught that life is a sacred trust for which everyone must answer in the final day of judgment when "Every one of us shall give account of himself to God." (Romans 14:12.) The Bible establishes patterns and principles of excellence also in Proverbs 3:33: "The curse of the Lord is in the house of the wicked: but he blesseth the habitation of the just." When young people are taught to train their vision on biblical goals, they will find no time, place, or inclination to become involved with narcotics, alcohol, or other temptations.

2. A youngster must be taught and encouraged to choose wholesome companions. Except for persons who have become hooked by accident or as a result of pain-killing medication, it is difficult to find a case of addiction among young people that was not induced by association with the wrong kind of companions. Youngsters should be encouraged to bring friends home for supervised activities and they should be guided to the kinds of places where they will meet the sort of friends they would be proud to bring home with them. These friends can be found at church or synagogue, in scouting, at religious

camps, and the like. They are not likely to be found in billiard parlors or on street corners.

3. A youngster should be guided into the proper choice of free-time activities. The youth who is seriously interested in school and keeps busy in extracurricular affairs or an after-school job seldom becomes involved with the kinds of people who are likely to drag him into addiction. The dangerous periods are after school, during vacations, and over long week ends. It is a parental duty to see to it that children have little time for unplanned or unchaperoned social activities, particularly at these times.

It is never too late, or too early, to help youngsters not yet in trouble or already in serious difficulty. Prevention offers the most realistic antidote for the narcotics traffic until such time as our law-enforcement agencies stop dragging their feet and really try to do something to stamp it out. Meanwhile, the most effective kind of prevention we have found so far lies in changing the home environment through education, beginning at birth, that is designed to teach self-reliance, the ability to face problems and crises squarely, and the courage to say No, even if it makes one unpopular.

The child who is loved and disciplined lovingly and who learns that his tensions can be dissipated if he is able to solve his own problems has armor against the assaults of the world's temptations. Parents must teach children how to deal with failure and disappointment, success and victory—to be good winners and better losers. They should help children learn to make choices between that which is safe and right and honest and that which is dangerous and wrong and dishonest—and to make these choices independently, not under the influence of what the Jones boy next door is doing.

If there is faith in the home and if the family practices what it preaches, moral values are certain to be upgraded. It is unfortunately true that the squalor of slums, with their broken homes and absentee parents, is more likely to produce juvenile dope addicts than is affluent suburbia, but we have seen that a growing number of sons of the well-to-do are becoming involved. Regardless of how many rooms there are in a house and how filled they are with possessions, regardless of the parents' status in the community, their children need help in learning how to make choices on the basis of moral standards. I daresay there is no more prayer and Bible-reading in suburbia than the slums—perhaps even less.

Most important, parents who have done their best to raise their children under the banner of God need never fear this invasion of addiction. I have *never* met a drug addict whose parents had succeeded in instilling sound spiritual precepts in his life.

# 8

## Homosexuality Starts at Home

Homosexuality is one of the greatest social problems of our modern world. When I first came to New York City, I did not grasp its full significance, but after nearly a decade of counseling with homosexuals and trying to understand their problems, and after accepting many of them in residence as patients at our centers, I have become acutely aware of some of the more tragic aspects of this deviation. At one time we accepted as patients male and female homosexuals who also were addicts, hoping to break all their bad habits at once. We abandoned this double therapy, however, because few homosexuals addicted to narcotics wanted to overcome their abnormality. An addict would tell me, "I want to kick the junk habit, I want to stop drinking, but I still want to be 'gay.'" Out of more than five hundred homosexuals I interviewed, only ten indicated that they actually wanted help.

One of our more dramatic cases was that of Mary Rich, an

attractive girl of twenty-one who was brought to me by her
mother shortly after she had served a sentence for addiction.
Mrs. Rich was followed into my office by Mary and an
extremely obese, sloppy, dirty girl about the same age. They
were holding hands, and it was clear that Mrs. Rich did not
care for their behavior.

"Look at my girl," she said. "She's bad. She's on narcotics
and runs around with the wrong crowd. I don't seem to be
able to help her. I help other kids on the street, but I've got a
bad one myself."

Mary sneered, just as George and his brother had, and
refused to talk with me as long as her mother was present. As
in the case of the minister-father who had visited me with his
two boys, I asked Mrs. Rich to leave. Both girls remained, and
I observed them closely. There was no doubt in my mind
about their relationship, but I decided to ask them bluntly if
my conclusion was accurate. "It's none of your business," the
fat girl said and left the room. Once alone with Mary, it was
not difficult to talk to her. She admitted that she had established
the relationship while she was in jail. It startled me to hear her
say she would rather die than give up her friend. She hated her
mother, she said, because she devoted her life as a missionary
to helping teen-agers but had not really got through to her
own daughter. It was the case of the distraught minister all
over again.

In talking to Mary, I learned that when she was a teen-ager,
she would come home from school to find her mother had
been so busy saving souls that she had not bothered to prepare
supper. The house was unkempt and there was no communication between mother and daughter. Mary turned first to
narcotics and then, in jail, she found this new relationship,

which gave her the acceptance and love she had craved from her mother.

I was indignant when I heard this and offered to pray for her. Mary just laughed and said, "Reverend, you can throw the devil out of me, and I'll walk right out in the hall and leave with my friend." And that is what happened—but she did not leave until I had warned her that she would go to jail again, that she would lose her friend, and that eventually she *would* cry for help, possibly when it was to late.

A week passed. Mrs. Rich called me at two o'clock one morning and said, "Mary is in jail again and she wants help. Would you please visit her?" The next day two girls on our staff visited Mary in jail and found her desperate, pleading for this help. It was, indeed, too late, for she was already headed for trial and a long term in jail.

I have thought often about this girl because hers is a problem shared by thousands of teen-agers, male and female, in cities large and small. Whether people admit it or not, the problem is there. This was pointed up sharply on a visit I made to a moderate-sized Southern city to conduct a youth crusade. When I arrived at the airport, I was met by a reporter whose first question was, "Have you come to our city to clean it up?" I replied, "No, I have come here to warn the parents of teen-agers about the problems that invade communities and to tell them how to avoid them." The reporter looked at me skeptically and told me that his city did not have narcotics or homosexuality problems and that the subjects I planned to discuss at my meetings applied only to large metropolitan areas such as New York, Los Angeles, and Chicago. I did not argue with him, deciding to wait and see what happened.

My service that evening was attended by more than one

thousand youngsters. Afterward three girls approached me and asked if they could speak to me. I took them aside and sat down with them. Gradually their story came out. It had all started when they were browsing at a downtown newsstand, where they bought paperback books containing sordid tales about homosexuality. This led them to experimenting, and now they were unable to stop what they had begun. The girls told me that there were homosexual rings in five high schools in their city and that the blight was spreading. They were worried lest their parents find out. What should they tell their mothers and fathers when they asked why they had lost so much weight, why their grades were slipping, and why they did not go out with boys any more? I referred them to a local pastor for counseling, since they clearly wanted help; I have since received several hopeful reports on their progress.

This sort of thing has happened in almost every city in which I have conducted a youth rally. Once, in Boston, where I appeared on a radio program during which members of the audience telephoned questions that were broadcast, I was told by a young caller that he attended a high school where the students had designated each Thursday as "queers day," at which time all boys and girls so inclined wore orange so they could recognize one another. I have heard of this being done in other cities as well.

For parents or ministers who would suggest that I am overstating the extent of this problem, I think you should know that I prevented two young people from committing suicide because they could not cope with this influence upon their lives. I will tell you about one of these episodes. It involved a nineteen-year-old girl who had been accepted at

one of our Teen Challenge centers. She had tried unsuccess-
fully for three months to rid her mind of the horrible guilt
associated with her activities. In her despair, she decided that
suicide was the only way out. She locked herself in a bathroom, found a razor blade in the medicine chest, and slashed
her wrists, screaming and cursing as she did so. I waited an
agonizing fifteen minutes while two of our boys broke the
door open. It took all of my strength to pry the razor blade out
of the girl's hand as she tried to slash me. That bleeding,
hysterical girl who could not break a habit that she did not
really understand made me realize that society, particularly the
church, must face up to this problem and offer some kind of
help, if not a solution.

*Please take heed.* This is a problem that threatens to involve
more and more of our children. It is because of the seriousness
of it that I have included this chapter on homosexuality. It will
not offer an easy solution because there is none. But perhaps
we can at least shed a little light on the subject by indicating
what the Bible says is the cause, and suggesting that the
church must believe and preach that there can be hope for
homosexuals.

The rise of homosexuality among our youth is one of the
major failures of American home life. It may even become
one of the major failures of American civilization. There was
a time when people tended to believe that the homosexual was
born that way, that he was not a product of his environment.
Now it is generally agreed that, except in the rarest of instances, the human shortcoming that contributed to the downfall of Greece and Rome is a result of childhood experience,
often fomented by a too-doting mother and a disinterested or

negligent father (with perhaps the reverse true in the case of Lesbians), but also nurtured by a society that increasingly indicates acceptance of this aberration.

When we first began seeing overt homosexuals at our centers, I thought I had better do a little research on the subject. I went to some of the foremost reference books as well as to other sources for information. What I learned gave me quite an education.

"Homosexuality is a problem as old as the world," an eminent psychiatrist said, "yet it is now so extensive it bears comparison to the decline and fall of the Roman Empire."

The statistical sources I consulted reported there are at least eleven homosexual organizations in the United States. No one knows exactly how many homosexuals there are, of course, but the estimates run as high as 15,000,000, with 400,000 to 500,000 of them believed to be in New York City alone. The late Dr. Alfred C. Kinsey, in his famous sex survey, maintained that 37 per cent of all American men had latent homosexual tendencies and one out of twenty-five was a practicing homosexual. Lesbianism, he said, claimed from one third to one half as many people as male homosexuality.

But you don't have to talk numbers to know that the problem is increasing. Just look around you wherever you go. For every flagrant homosexual you see, there may be scores of hidden, or underground, members of the "third sex" who seem on the surface to be perfectly normal. Some of these people prey on the youngster with latent tendencies, and it is important to be alert to them and their wiles.

There was a time when we ministers pretended homosexuality did not exist. Now the church is being forced to take a long look at this social cancer. It is interesting to note that while many church members have refused to recognize homosexuality, the Bible speaks clearly about the matter. First, there is grave spiritual danger. God's word is very clear on the subject. "Thou shalt not lie with mankind, as with womankind: it is an abomination," it says in Leviticus 18:22. And, "Wherefore God also gave them up to uncleanness through the lusts of their own hearts, to dishonour their own bodies between themselves: Who changed the truth of God into a lie, and worshipped and served the creature more than the Creator. . . . For this cause God gave them up into vile affections: for even their women did change the natural use into that which is against nature: And likewise also the men, leaving the natural use of the woman, burned in their lust one toward another; men with men working that which is unseemly, and receiving in themselves that recompence of their error which was meet" (Romans 1:24–27).

Doctors warn of other very real dangers in homosexuality. The most threatening is potential suicide. Judge John M. Murtagh, a distinguished New York jurist, in his book *Cast the First Stone,* said that probably 50 per cent of all suicides and homicides in a big city can be attributed to homosexuality. Other authorities agree, adding that the homosexual's life is characterized by deep loneliness, desperation, guilt, and frustration. Also, because they are never really fulfilled they are constantly seeking new thrills, which can lead to their becoming masochists or sadists. Crimes of arson and theft often have been linked directly to homosexuality. There is always the danger of alcoholism. One psychologist has gone so far as to say, "Not every alcoholic is homosexual, but every homosexual is alcoholic."

Venereal disease is another danger. Many people, mainly

youngsters, are under the misapprehension that venereal diseases cannot be contracted in a homosexual act. Dr. George James, while New York City Health Commissioner, said that, on the contrary, in New York alone 3,500 new cases of venereal disease were reported among young people eighteen or under in a single year, "and it is safe to say that for every one reported, two were not reported—and that those two were cases of venereal disease contracted by young people consorting with older homosexuals."

Civic leaders in New York regarded the threat as so dangerous that they published a thirty-two-page "comic" book warning youth of the threat. This was done after the venereal disease rate had jumped 56 per cent. A number of doctors blamed homosexual encounters, pointing out that the deviate is a sure carrier of disease because he uses no precautions and is constantly seeking new partners.

Without doubt, the greatest threat that homosexuals impose upon our society is the seduction of children. Krafft-Ebing states in *Psychopathia Sexualis* that seduction of the young is something the homosexual cannot resist. One need only read of the "gay" life to see the truth in this. The homosexual is constantly seeking someone young and "untouched." The tragedy is that most of those seduced are either led into a life of homosexuality or are seriously damaged psychologically by such an encounter.

The homosexual societies are frank in saying what they want from the general public. As listed in their publications, their demands include: permission to serve in the armed forces; acceptance in government jobs; recognition of marriages between members of the same sex with tax exemptions and the same status as for marriages between men and women; permission to adopt children; an end to prohibitions on realistic representation of homosexual life on television and in literature and movies; recognition of homosexual love by the church; permission for homosexuals to dress as they please; freedom of the homosexual press to print what it chooses; and the liberty to make advances to any persons they find attractive.

The very nature of these demands indicates what is so terribly wrong with homosexuality. It demonstrates the threat of the "third sex" to our society and perhaps to our entire civilization.

Why do we have homosexuals living in their own separate world? Diagnosis certainly is no cure, but to understand the homosexual, to help him and to save others from plunging into this twilight world, we need to know at least some of the causes, which appear to be both sociological and psychological.

At least one cause for the rise in homosexuality is the increase in the feminization of men and the masculinization of women. The presence of women in the highly competitive business and professional worlds is one factor. Hair styles are a good index; young men with long hair and girls with short cuts, for example. Fashions in clothes are involved, too, psychologists agree. Not long ago, writing in *The New York Post,* Ruth Preston asked, "Is there a creeping femininity in men's fashions?" James Laver, the English fashion historian, says, "Clothes of both sexes are approaching one another so closely that in districts like London's Chelsea it is impossible to tell from the back which of a trousered pair is the man and which the woman. Especially, if the man wears long hair, which most of the 'far-out boys' do." A manufacturer, George Richman,

thought the trend sufficiently alarming to call a news conference and warn against the "femme fads" and the "hand-on-
hip" fashions that were becoming popular. These styles, com-
mentaries of our age, are some of the social factors that
contribute to the spread of homosexuality.

One of the more significant sociological factors is the permissive attitude of the entertainment industry toward homosexuality, and toward all other sexual activity as well. The
homosexual theme is explored quite frankly on the screen, in
novels, on television, and on the stage, and several recent best-
sellers have homosexual heroes. More subtle is the demorali-
zation of marriage and the heterosexual relationship in much
of our drama and fiction. Marriage is frequently portrayed as
a trap that robs each partner of freedom and happiness. The
heterosexual relationship is described in such works in vulgar
language. The female is the aggressor while the male is
passive. The wife is unfaithful and nagging, reduced to an
immoral animal seething with sexual desires and cruel im-
pulses. The young men—and young women—in the audience
may begin to distrust the opposite sex if they are subjected to
this kind of fare, and if they believe what they see and hear. It
seems perfectly natural for some to turn to members of their
own sex after such public and extensive exposure to homosexuality, much of which is initiated by homosexual writers, to
say nothing of producers, directors, and performers.

The philosopher Nietzsche reminds us, "When there are no
longer men, the women will become men." At the time this
happens, our society will crumble. The burning of draft cards
is an indication that too many of our young men would rather
be part of a soft society than become real men fighting for
freedom. If you consider what happened in Greece and Rome,

you would have cause for concern. When Rome first conquered Greece, the Greek sculpture was predominantly feminine—as were many of its young men. At that time, Roman sculpture reflected the virility and power of manhood. Six centuries later, however, just before the barbarian hordes invaded Rome, the sculpture had become feminized, reflecting what had happened to many Roman men. It was Greece all over again. The softening of the empire's manhood was the prelude to downfall, bearing out Aristotle's comment, "A country is only as strong as each man in it and its civilization only as great as its dreams."

There are, of course, deep personal as well as sociological reasons for homosexuality. In some cases, psychological factors contribute far more than do sociological influences. At the outset of this discussion, I said that homosexuals are made, not born. Homosexuality begins in the cradle, not in the womb. It is the parents who must accept the primary responsibility for what happens to a newborn child. Early rejection of a baby can form lifelong impressions that are difficult if not impossible to erase. The parents who are disappointed at having a son because they wanted a daughter, or the reverse, can blight a child's entire life if they make this feeling obvious, as many do. From the crib through the formative years, love and acceptance are essential. Dr. Clyde M. Narramore, in his excellent book, *The Psychology of Counseling,* says the following types of parents can contribute to the creation of tendencies toward sexual deviation in a child.

*The dominant mother.* She stifles her son's masculinity, causing him to lose confidence in his own sex. He fears all women because of his mother and dreads the thought of intimacy with any woman. She may compete with her son for the father's attention and tell the child he was an "unwanted" baby. She says she planned for a daughter, dresses the boy in frills, insists that he play with girls, and subconsciously tries to make him fill the role of a daughter. By the time he reaches maturity, he finds it natural to play the role of a girl. The reverse sometimes happens to a girl. She was supposed to be a boy, so she is given a boy's name, and so on. Here the dominant father can be an influence toward Lesbianism.

*The weak father.* Real tragedy results when a dominant mother is paired with a weak father. The son cannot look to his father for support in his struggle to be a man. The daughter loses respect for all men because of her father and is psychologically seduced by the masculine mother. Sexual identification is lost, and the child becomes confused.

*The over-indulgent mother.* Just as harmful as the dominant mother is the one who caters to every whim of her son. She spoils him and when he is small may take him to bed with her when the father is away or relations are strained. Psychologically she seduces the child and tries to make him a substitute for her husband. Attachment between mother and son thus may grow to be very strong, so strong that he cannot break away. In many cases, the father is not much help. The boy feels, "Why get married? No girl could ever measure up to my mother." The thought of a normal sexual relationship seems repellent—"That would be like having sexual relations with my mother." Then, too, such mothers may tend to picture sex as something that is dirty and unnatural. They may complain about the pain of childbirth. Thus the door to heterosexual relationships is gradually shut and homosexuality results. Girls, too, can drift into homosexuality under the influence of such mothers, who make sex and childbirth seem unpleasant and who use daughters as buffers to keep their husbands at bay.

*The cruel father.* A son's fear of competition with other men can result from having a cruel father who subjects the boy to physical or mental punishment. A child has a deep wish to be accepted by members of his own sex, particularly his parent, and once a boy's father rejects him, he will turn to other males. He learns as he grows older that one way to win acceptance in the male world is to let other men use his body. Such youths are easy prey for older homosexuals, and once the pattern is established, it is very difficult to break. The daughter of such a father becomes afraid of men because of his cruelty. She may see herself in the role of the abused mother. Her fear of her father is transferred to all men. Since girls, like boys, crave love, she turns to members of her own sex.

Other doctors have offered additional reasons for homosexual behavior. It has been suggested that one unnatural sexual experience or one unsatisfactory normal sexual adventure can lead one into homosexuality. It would seem, however, that if the individual seduced into the ways of the third sex had no latent tendencies in that direction, the pattern of behavior would never have developed in the first place.

There are those who insist that genetic or glandular differences are the causes. Research on this has indicated, however, that glandular functions affect the power of sex but are not likely to determine the direction. Heredity, it appears, has little or nothing to do with homosexuality. One may point to certain overt homosexuals and say, But they have all the characteristics. What is not taken into consideration is the fact that there are many others who do not appear outwardly to be homosexuals and yet indeed are. It is difficult to generalize about what a homosexual looks and acts like, since the only ones we can be sure of are those who make their homosexuality evident because they apparently want the world to know what they are.

My conclusion, as a result of talks with psychologists and extensive reading on the subject, is that children reared in strong, happy homes will not grow up to become homosexuals, just as they will not grow up to become narcotics addicts or criminals, despite the sociological pressures closing in on them. Thus an enormous responsibility is heaped on parents: Those who find a son or daughter heading for or already involved in homosexual activity should refrain from asking, What is wrong with *him?* and inquire instead, What is wrong with *us?* What did *we* do that was wrong? How can we help this child? A leading authority on the homosexual problem commented recently that "the real tragedy of homosexuality is that with a little understanding, love and help from the parents of these victims this would not have happened at all."

It is not necessarily true that once a youth has become a homosexual, *nothing* can be done about it, but it is true that the rate of "cure" is very low. Everyone who has tried to help homosexuals—psychiatrists, psychologists, and pastoral counselors—is in agreement that theirs is a very difficult pattern to change. But there are cases in which homosexuals have made readjustments that have enabled them to marry and have children and, most important, abandon their homosexual ways. The chief difficulty we encounter is *the large number who do not want to change.* They like the way they are! At least that is what they say. One cannot read their literature without becoming acutely aware that they feel theirs is a superior way of life. They point proudly to the great artistic contributions of homosexuals and tend to equate fame with homosexuality, portraying only homosexuals as great artists, musicians, actors, and writers. However, I noted with interest recently the results of a series of psychological tests that showed that the degree of talent, creativity, and contribution is much higher among persons with normal sexual relationships than among homosexuals.

I was present recently when a homosexual was asked if he wanted to be cured. "Cured of what?" he asked. "There is nothing wrong with me." When another young man was fired from his job because of his deviation, he declared, "That's just the way I am and you will have to accept me this way."

It seems obvious that if the cure for homosexuality is difficult, we should devote our efforts to preventive action. There are strong guidelines in the Scriptures that could help stem the rising tide of homosexuality if we would but put them to work. Parents who want to dress a boy in girls' clothing might find guidance in Deuteronomy 22:5: "The woman shall not wear that which pertaineth unto a man, neither shall a man put on a woman's garment: for all that do so are abomination unto the Lord thy God." And some of our long-haired beatniks could learn from I Corinthians 11:14,15: "Doth not even nature itself teach you, that, if a man have long hair, it is a shame unto him? But if a woman have long hair, it is a glory to her: for her hair is given her for a covering."

Parents should read I Peter 3 and Ephesians 5 and 6. Keeping in mind the causes of homosexuality, note what Peter says about a proper marriage relationship: Wives should be in subjection to their own husbands; women should be meek and quiet of spirit; husbands are to give honor unto the wife as the weaker vessel, to respect her and hold her in high esteem; both are to be of one mind, with compassion, love, pity, and courtesy for the other. When reading this, bear in mind that Peter was a married man.

Add to this the words of Paul in Ephesians: Women again are to be in subjection, with men the head of the house; husbands are told to love their wives as their own bodies; the wife is to revere the husband; children are to obey and honor their parents; parents are to deserve that honor by not provoking them to wrath through misunderstanding, lack of appreciation, or neglect; and finally, the children are to be brought up in the fear and admonition of the Lord.

The Bible allows no room for the dominant mother, the weak father, the overindulgent mother, or the cruel father. Thus, if these admonitions are followed by parents, their children will have a good chance to grow up and be normal human beings.

Now, what about the person already involved in the homosexual life? Shall we give up on him? Shall we tell ourselves that we can do nothing and therefore ignore him? I say No. Perhaps we will not be able to cure him, but we certainly can help him. The very least we can do is try. We must begin by trying to develop a complete understanding of his problem. Parents should seek the help of professional counselors in trying to determine the cause. The young homosexual should be encouraged to see the counselor, who in turn should not allow himself to become overly impressed by mere confessions or even deep contrition; both of these reactions are normal ones for the homosexual during a course of counseling. It is to be expected also that there will be periods of regression. The important thing is to determine whether the person really wants help. If he does, he has a chance; if he doesn't, nothing is likely to change him.

How do you go about determining if the homosexual really wants to change? First, did he seek help voluntarily? Or was he caught and sent by the police or court officials, or pressured into counseling by his frantic family? If he comes voluntarily, possibly with the *encouragement and support* of his family, he really does want help. I would expect also the person to be willing and ready to confess fully to God, without casting any blame for his plight on his parents or friends. He must be willing to break all ties with former companions, regardless of how close they might have been.

Perhaps it will be considered wise during the course of talks between a troubled young person and his counselor to call in one or both parents for private conversations. Sometimes a parent can help to alleviate a homosexual's anxiety if he talks out the problem with an expert and makes an honest effort to determine what he did to contribute to his child's sexual deviation and how he can deal with his own guilt. Probably the biggest contribution parents can make when a son or daughter is trying to fight his way into the normal sexual world is to demonstrate his love and understanding by being sympathetic and patient.

I must caution parents: Fewer than 25 per cent of all homosexuals display overt symptoms. Most knowledgeable people in this field agree that there is no positive way to discern every homosexual or potential deviate, since most of them camouflage themselves in cloaks of seeming normality.

Also it must be emphasized that many normal men and women who display some of the characteristics are in no danger of becoming homosexual.

To end this discussion on a positive note, I would like to take a page from the Scriptures. In I Corinthians, 6:9–11, Paul the Apostle, in a letter to the Corinthians, testifies that some of them had been delivered from a variety of sins, including homosexuality:

"Know ye not that the unrighteous shall not inherit the kingdom of God? Be not deceived: neither fornicators, nor idolators, nor adulterers, *nor effeminate, nor abusers of themselves with mankind,* nor thieves, nor covetous, nor drunkards, nor revilers, nor extortioners, shall inherit the kingdom of God. And such *were* some of you: but ye are washed, but ye are sanctified, but ye are justified in the name of the Lord Jesus, and by the Spirit of our God."

# 9

## The "Other Half" of Illegitimacy

Harry was a scrawny kid, not quite sixteen, and he had not even begun to shave. He fumbled with the letter opener on my desk and frowned. After a few moments his face relaxed into a slightly silly grin and he said: "I don't know exactly why I did it. I guess I was trying to prove I was a man."

In the course of "proving" his manhood, Harry had fathered an illegitimate child, but once he had performed the act that had created this new life, he was not man enough to accept what he had done. He wanted nothing further to do with the girl, for whom *he* had lost respect. She had been his steady date in high school. They had necked and petted for a long time. Harry's friends kept asking him if they had "gone all the way," and they taunted him as a square when he said No.

Finally, Harry managed to make his girl feel that if she declined him, she would be doubting his manhood, so she and Harry engaged in sexual intercourse regularly for a few weeks until she discovered she was pregnant. After that, he wanted nothing more to do with her and even threatened her with public disgrace if she told his father and mother.

I concluded when I talked with the girl that it was not all Harry's fault. These disasters seldom can be blamed on only one person. She had a craving for affection, which, she said, she had never received at home, so she eventually took this way to satisfy this particular need in her life without really knowing why. Harry's plea for his manhood was just an excuse and not the reason for her compliance. Ironically, neither she nor Harry particularly enjoyed their sexual experiences. *Something* was lacking every time. Both acknowledged that their relationship had been unsatisfactory and at times embarrassing, but that once they had started they simply did not know how to stop. And they had not thought of using contraceptives, for like many other young people, they felt that "taking precautions" would make it sex for sex's sake, and their emotions were "above that."

You can see that these youngsters, like many others, were too immature to deal with the facts of life or with the events that followed. The baby was put out for adoption shortly after birth without being seen by either parent. The girl's mother and father were ashamed, not so much because their daughter had engaged in illicit sex but because she had become pregnant as a result!

They sent her away to have the baby and refused to accept her at home again for a long time after that for fear people would suspect why she had been absent. Harry's guilt developed slowly and now he is coming to Teen Challenge for help because he does not want to get a girl into trouble again. He has discussed his problems with his parents, too, and they are giving him considerable sympathetic support now that they have come to realize that his deficiencies in values were largely their fault.

Why should we bother with Harry and other unwed fathers? Aren't they simply doing what comes naturally for a boy? Why should they be blamed? After all, isn't it always the girl's fault for not saying No? What harm can pregnancy possibly do to a boy, who has nothing to hide? These are questions we hear frequently. However, in the case of unwed parents, there can be as many as six people to blame—the youngsters, of course, and also, the parents of both.

About 250,000 children are born to unwed mothers in our country every year, and at least one of every six American brides is pregnant when she marries. I suspect the figures actually are much higher because many cases are kept secret. In addition, it has been said that a minimum of one million illegal abortions are performed in the United States every year—perhaps far more. For every one of these, there has to be a boy *and* a girl, a man *and* a woman. Most illegitimacies, by the way, involve adults, with teen-agers accounting for perhaps 25 to 30 per cent of the total number of babies born out of wedlock. If the example of a New England high school is any indication, this ratio may be changing, however. Officials of the school reported that twenty girls had to drop out in one year because of pregnancy. The following year, the figure jumped to fifty-two, and this in a school with a total student population of about 1,300!

In past generations, the stigma of illegitimacy has been pinned by society on the unwed mother, with the father remaining unidentified and therefore ignored. This is not entirely true any more, although the scarlet letter still is figuratively affixed to the mother, and one seldom, if ever, hears a censorious word directed at the men who father children out of wedlock. Increasing efforts are being made, however, to reach the fathers and help them see that part of the burden of responsibility and guilt is theirs. The preventive advantages of dealing with unwed fathers—or even potential unwed fathers—is obvious, for if a boy's sense of moral values can be improved, his chances of engaging in illicit sex will be reduced.

We—and I'm sure others who work with troubled youngsters—have found that unwed fathers, mainly those still in their teens, have serious problems and that this anti-social behavior is but a symptom of deep-seated difficulty. These boys need help. Their plight certainly cannot match in intensity that of the girl who has to leave town and enter a maternity home to hide her evidence from society, but the unwed father does need to be reached. This was demonstrated in Philadelphia, where the Youth Study Center of the Juvenile Division of the County Court conducted individual counseling sessions with teen-age unmarried fathers. The counseling was provided because the boys obviously were struggling with severe problems often concealed under thin shells of mock bravado and brazen conduct. The longer the counseling lasted, the less boastful the boys became. Eventually many of them became obviously bewildered and self-reproachful.

The Philadelphia authorities found that more than 85 per cent of the boys came from homes where the mothers were the dominating factors or where there were no fathers at all. Many of these boys, by becoming fathers outside of marriage, were able to reproduce the desertions of their own fathers. In a report on this program, one boy was quoted as saying, "My baby will grow up wondering who was his father, like I've always wondered. He'll think I didn't love him and he'll hate me." Most of the boys said they were willing to "marry the girl," but less out of love than a need to keep the child from growing up to hate his father. Many were said to be angry because the unwed mother received all the attention, and one was recorded as saying, "Nobody lets us say how we feel about this. They look at the girl's big belly and they think the girl is the only one who has got a problem."

Just how much the unwed father needs help was illustrated to me in this letter I received from a teen-age boy:

". . . I heard you speak in Los Angeles about teen-age sex morals. I think you're an old-fashioned prune. There is nothing wrong with having sex and going all the way when two are really in love. Your ideas went out with the Model T Ford. I have sex twice a week and am planning to marry B____ when I'm 20 or 21. Why don't you stick to helping addicts? J.M., Santa Cruz, Calif."

And here is another:

". . . I'll tell you why we teen-agers grab a fifth of whisky and crawl into bed with a girl. . . . You parents have started a war in Viet Nam. You've set a terrible example regarding morals and honesty and you expect us to be angels. We are only copying from you. . . . Don't preach what you know you don't practice. . . . Good luck, preacher. John C., Wilmington, Del."

And,

". . . My father is a deacon in the _____ church. He has no idea that I am involved with 15 other kids in a sex ring. It is not just a non-virgin club. We read erotic books, we tear out the best scenes and paste them in our scrap book and then recite them to each other. None of our debs has been pregnant and they are out of the club if they get caught by someone out of the group. . . . It all started with two books, C____ and P____. Dan Y., Toronto, Canada."

It would not surprise me if these boys became unwed fathers. I would not be surprised either to see any of them on our Teen Challenge doorstep some day. Dealing with illegitimacy is a kind of by-product of our work with young people. At Teen Challenge, our primary function is to help narcotics addicts, delinquents, and others in trouble. Many times we encounter illegitimacy as well, and so we have learned to cope with this problem as it arises. We do not pretend to be experts, but we are learning fast. We have to in our kind of work, especially when we encounter teen-gang members who think that one of the badges of manhood is to "have a kid." It has been painful for me to observe puny little adolescents look admiringly at a gang leader and say with envy, "He's got a kid!" Sometimes during an interview with an addict or a delinquent, there will be a pause while he tries to remember how many girls he has impregnated. One boy will say, "Let me see—two—or maybe—let's see—no—three kids." Another says, "How do I know? Quite a few, I'll bet."

Sometimes statutory rape charges are filed against boys who get girls in trouble, and the boys are justifiably bitter about this. I have been in court with boys charged with statutory rape who have complained that the girls led them on. "Look, preacher," one boy said. "They nail me for rape and I'll get locked up. See that girl sitting over there with her mother. She looks innocent now, but you should have seen her when we were in the back seat of my car. She ain't no angel." Actually no one knows who the guilty party is in cases such as this.

Both are at fault in most situations. And their parents also must share the guilt. We always try very hard to persuade boys to acknowledge their fatherhood of an illegitimate child, but fear of rape charges often makes it difficult to get this admission.

When a boy admits he has been involved, or when a girl can identify the boy who got her into trouble, we make every effort to counsel both of them. We subscribe to the theory developed in Southern California by Reuben Pannor, who has pioneered in work with unwed fathers at the Vista Del Mar Child Care Service, that efforts to help the boys involved must accompany attempts to assist the unwed mothers, and sometimes the parents of both youngsters should be called on, too. Pannor says, and we agree, that any agency or church that does not include "the other half" of illegitimacy is making an inadequate approach to the problem.

We at Teen Challenge have taken a lesson from Pannor's book by insisting that all teen-age unmarried fathers who come to us must tell their parents what has happened. The boys do not like to do this because their parents usually react by becoming angry, and sometimes considerable time must elapse before they simmer down to an understanding mood. But the parents are often as much to blame for what has happened as the boy—although indirectly, of course—and therefore should share in his responsibility. Sometimes we can help parents see where they have made mistakes and convince them that it takes real courage to set limits for children's behavior. Going steady, for example, should be discouraged. Young people need to be involved in more group social activities instead of slipping off to be alone in parked cars. They may find out about the facts of life from books, teachers, or friends, but they need to be able to relate what they learn to life. They must learn from their parents about the *feelings* and *responsibilities* that accompany the right kind of sex. Only then will their outlooks and behavior change.

Interestingly, in all the research I have done among teenagers and in our work at Teen Challenge, I have observed how few cases of illegitimacies there are among youngsters from homes with strong religious beliefs and where the children receive religious training. This has been reported at Reuben Pannor's center. Also, a recent study showed that only one of a number of unwed mothers came from homes where at least one parent attended a church. Moreover, every girl in a group in which there had been no illegitimacies said at least one parent regularly went to church and most of the girls themselves were churchgoers. We would not want anyone to regard religion as a cure-all, of course, but it appears to be a factor in the passing of moral values from one generation to another.

Here, too, it is essential that parents set proper examples and show that they adapt moral values to their own lives and do not just talk about them. Unfortunately, young people often are simply imitating adult behavior without applying adult values to their acts, and are acting without an awareness of sex as the expression of love and mating in marriage.

What appears to be a rise in promiscuity among youngsters is a result of a sexual revolution that has been going on in our country for the nearly half a century since the end of World War I. Obviously the mass production of automobiles has had no small part to play in the new "sex freedom." Teen-age sexual activity most often takes place in parked cars, although it also occurs in parks and on benches, and amazingly, at home during the day when working mothers are away. Accompanying the automobile boom and prosperity in general has been a decline in the traditional values and authority of the family, community, and church as well as an increase in individual freedom of decision and action, which has been extended to children, too. The fact that an individual may be only fifteen or sixteen years old in no way seems to limit his freedom.

The permissive parents I have criticized throughout this book appear to be afraid to block their children lest they lose their love, and some adults are so preoccupied with their own problems they often say Yes just to get a child out of the way. Oddly enough, permissive parents also often become overprotective, in a way, to demonstrate their love. I'm talking about the parents who foot the bills for acts of juvenile vandalism and hush up automobile accidents involving their children. After being so indulgent, these parents become shocked and angry when they learn their children have been experimenting with sex. What overindulged, overprotected child would not be confused—especially when the situation is compounded by the knowledge that his parents condone similar behavior in their friends and are sometimes guilty of illicit behavior themselves? One aspect of this attitude is found in the fact that many parents of unwed fathers and mothers seem to be more ashamed and upset over the *pregnancy* than over the fact their children have been engaging in illicit sex. They apparently do not care what goes on as long as there are no unfortunate results. I was shocked when the mother of a teen-age girl said to me recently, "I don't care what she does in the back seat of her boy friend's car. I just don't want her to come home pregnant. That's why I've taught her to use protection."

Illicit sex is an outgrowth of our "fun morality," as portrayed in movies and on television, in novels and on the stage, in advertisements and in songs—and in tolerant discussions by parents during dinner about the extramarital lives of some of their friends. There is an emphasis on sex in advertising that is distressing indeed, especially when you hear a teen-age girl in her seventh month of pregnancy say, "You grow up believing that if you buy the right bra, happiness is sure to be yours. Well, I tried it and look at me today."

Let me tell you about another girl. I met her while I was conducting a youth rally in Pittsburgh after giving one of my favorite sermons, "Parked at the Gates of Hell." In this sermon, I relate the Bible story (II Samuel 13) about Prince Amnon and Princess Tamar, who got in "trouble" because they mistook lust for love. Part of my message to the five thousand teen-agers at the rally went something like this:

"Here was a young man with a good background who ruined the life of a beautiful princess by pretending he truly loved her. That, he believed, made seduction all right. He fooled the girl's parents and laid a trap into which she walked with eyes wide open. Like most girls who are 'forced' into sexual intercourse, she knew what was on his mind and could have run away in time. But, encouraged by her flirtatiousness, he seized her and forced his attentions on her. Then he turned on her with hate and shame. The Bible says, 'Then Amnon hated her *exceedingly;* so that the hatred wherewith he hated her was greater than the love wherewith he had loved her. And Amnon said unto her, *Arise, be gone!*'

"This kind of tragic story is being told too often today about boys who, after they have indulged their appetites, turn on girls and despise and forsake them."

After my sermon, several hundred girls and boys responded to my call to "confess and clean up." Among them was a very pretty sixteen-year-old blonde who clutched my coat sleeve to get my attention.

"Please let me talk to you! I am in real trouble," she cried.

As soon as I could, I took her backstage, where she poured out her story.

"Three months ago, I thought I was in real trouble," she said. "I was going steady with one of the worst kids in my school and we were parking near a cemetery and having sex. All the time he kept warning me, 'I'm not using any protection. If you get knocked up, I'll never take you out again.' I don't know why I kept on going out with him, but I guess I was trying to get even with my mother for running around with other men when my father was away.

"Pretty soon I thought I was going to have a baby and I got scared. I never prayed so hard in my life. I made a deal with God. If He would get me out of trouble, I'd never try sex again until I was married and really in love."

By this time, the girl was sobbing and wringing her hands. I gave her my handkerchief and waited for her to compose herself enough to continue. "A miracle happened," she said, "and I found out I wasn't pregnant. I felt so relieved and happy, and everything was all right for a while. But then, a few weeks later, I started feeling lonely and forsaken again with no one at home to pay any attention to me, and I began to think about calling this boy, even though I knew what he wanted to do when we were together. I finally called him and he picked me up the next night and we went to our old spot. He turned on the radio and we heard a song that said, 'Love makes it all right.' He said he really loved me, and just like the song said, everything would turn out all right. This time, he said, 'If you get pregnant, I'll stick with you and we'll get married right away.'

"I'm pregnant now, for sure, but when I called him to tell him, he swore at me and said I was a fool. He doesn't want to see me any more. He just said, 'Tough luck, kid, that's the way things go,' and hung up on me."

The girl said she could not stay with her family because they refused to believe she was pregnant. She said she had thought about killing herself, and unless I could help her, she probably would. I sent her to a nearby shelter, where our workers tried to learn the name of the father of her unborn child, but she refused to identify him. She was so bitter about him she wanted nothing further to do with him. When I last heard from the girl, her child had been born and placed for adoption. The father of her child remains unknown to us— and unhelped.

Many girls have come to us in this same plight. What emerges from all of their stories is that they knew what they were doing when they submitted to their boy friends and were aware of the possible consequences of their actions. Such sexual irresponsibility is difficult to combat in a world in which parents, and even schools, exert increasing pressure for earlier and earlier maturity—going steady in the first grade and attending evening dances in the fourth. We even find flat-chested little girls bragging about their preteen bras, which make them feel as grown up as their big sisters. Parents constantly worry lest their youngsters will not be as popular as others, so they encourage overly busy social lives. That often means that a child, instead of developing standards, will do anything to make himself popular. Thus children, pushed by the demands of their parents and goaded constantly by erotic ads, movies, TV, magazines, and books, find themselves coping with problems of adolescence long before they actually are adolescents.

Harvey Cox, the theologian, has advanced several interesting thoughts on this subject. He points out that children today are accustomed to many things their parents had to wait to grow up for—trips to Europe, cars, smoking and drinking, and generous allowances. These experiences have made sex almost the only adult privilege not openly available to adolescents, he says, so it has become a means through which they can express their rebellion, independence, and what they regard as their maturity.

The youngsters themselves offer some interesting answers when we ask them why they engage in illicit sex. Girls and boys generally give pretty much the same answers. They are trying to win the acceptance they cannot get at home. They want to be popular. They are trying to act like adults without being fully aware of what is involved. One thing just leads to another. And so on. A boy may say, My friends do it, so why shouldn't I? or like Harry, How can I prove I am a man without sex experience? A girl may say, How should I act when a boy tells me he wants to prove he is a man? What should a girl do to be popular? And both ask, What should we do about our sex feelings?

These are difficult questions, but we must try to answer them to the best of our ability. In doing so, we have to consider several important factors. Youngsters talk about sex a lot, but apparently they are ignorant about the general functioning of the human body. They do not discuss their concern about sex with adults very much, and when they do they often are given inadequate answers. We must also deal with the attitude of the high school girls who, in their bull sessions, instead of discussing how to turn a boy down often talk instead about the danger of pregnancy and how they would break the news to their parents.

It is important also for parents and those of us who work with troubled teen-agers to try to make clear to them the implications of parenthood and the meaningfulness of love and sexual intercourse *in marriage*. We must tell them about the responsibilities of being parents and their responsibilities toward one another. Sex should be presented to youngsters as part of a total love relationship, not as a clutching for affection such as proved to be the downfall of Harry's girl. Georgia H. Seward put it very well when she said: "People in our competitive, individualized society have an exorbitant need of affection and reassurance. It is this need for human response rather than genuine sexual desire which leads them into the tense, clutching type of relationship so prevalent among us. Sexual possession of another somehow assures an individual and bulwarks his ego defenses, taking the place of a partnership based on mutual love."

The books on sex—and there are many good ones—are filled with such discussions, but books are not enough. The subject is taught in schools, too, but there must be something wrong with much of what is being taught to our children. Sex education can be very damaging if it is taught solely as a science, as it so often is. My children tell me that their teachers often volunteer their own personal ideas on the subject, and I gather from what is said that they often tend to create an aura of permissiveness. I insist, as do many others, that there must be a quality to sex education beyond lectures in biology and dissemination of information about "the pill."

"The pill" is potentially a great boon to mankind, but it is becoming the bane of those of us who have to rescue teen-agers from trouble. I have heard about mothers who have their doctors prescribe "the pill" for them and then proceed to give it to their daughters, so they will not have to worry when the girls go out on dates. Not only is this of potential physical danger to teen-age girls, who are acting on the advice of their mothers rather than their doctors, but think: What is it doing to their sense of moral values when sex is equated with taking pills? We—clergymen and parents—have a lot of serious thinking to do about this, and I mean today, right now!

My feelings on most of the sex education I have heard about are pretty negative, I admit. The way youngsters have described it to me gives me the impression that it tends to be entirely too vague, too permissive, and often too enticing in its presentation. A teacher in New Jersey told her class, for example, "It is not evil to engage in homosexual practices, if both parties are agreeable." As a parent, this causes me great concern. Comments such as this have helped to create a preoccupation with "sex talk" that spills over into lunch hours and other periods of the day. It amazes me to see the number of teen-agers who emerge from biology classes as "experts" on sex matters because they have learned more in school than their parents did about the functions of the glands and the process of procreation. But they do not know how to put out the fire after the first few kisses.

At least part of sex education belongs in the home and in the pastor's study. We need more ministers who will take the time for straight, frank talk about sex and about the role of religion in sex. Some parents I have talked with feel they cannot instruct their children in sexual behavior because they don't feel capable of explaining it. They hem and haw and make excuses and act as though children have no right to ask questions about sex. One mother I know told her daughter, "Don't ever mention sex to me again. You should respect your mother more than that. Don't embarrass me that way again." This breakdown of communications puts an unfair burden of responsibility on the child. It is part of our growing tendency to give our teen-agers, boys probably more than girls, too much choice at too early an age. A lot of boys make relatively good sums of money, which they spend as they choose. Boys have informed me that they go to their fathers for advice only to be told, "I'm busy right now. Ask me later," or "You're old enough to make your own decisions." These fathers do not understand that when they are asked for help, it usually is needed. The father who really loves his child and is concerned about him will take the time to give such advice.

Here is where the schools, particularly colleges and universities, also make mistakes. They are placing too great a burden of decision-making on the shoulders of students, some of whom have left home for the first time and need a transition from whatever parental authority there may have been to running their lives on their own.

During a recent lecture tour of college campuses, I was told by a young fraternity boy that "week ends are for sex." He said every member of his house engaged in sex on week ends that are very well and "very economically" organized. The oldest boy in the fraternity and his date check into a motel, where they remain an hour and then silently slip away with car lights out. Then another car pulls into the parking lot and its occupants go into the room for an hour. As many as six couples use a motel room in a single night, all for the price of one couple.

This is the practice of fraternity brothers on a large university campus. But I also learned about promiscuity in church-sponsored Bible colleges and training schools. The young people who tell me about this have no feelings of guilt later about having had extramarital sexual experience, but they do worry about some of their erotic experiments.

The widely publicized college week ends at beaches also involve considerable sexual activity in which partners are changed daily, if not more often. One young man told me, "We come here for one thing, and one thing only, sex, sex, sex. The idea is to have a new chick every night. Why else would we come to a place like this?"

I suspect it would be a relief to students if schools as well as parents would set stronger limits on behavior, which in turn might make it much easier for young people to make the right decisions and to develop the right habits. Proper supervision would indicate that someone is concerned about them, someone cares. Why not ban liquor on campuses and in fraternity houses? Why not introduce curfews, particularly for girls, requiring them to be in at a certain hour each night? Why not insist on chaperones at fraternity house parties? Wouldn't it be a good idea to police the motels fringing many college campuses? The college stage is a little late to reach many students who have not received moral and religious support at home, but perhaps it is not too late to help them learn that it is possible to say No. The ability to say No is one of the most difficult of self-disciplines, but once developed it can spare the individual and those about him much misery.

Although much of my own ministry is concerned with young people from underprivileged, impoverished homes, the young people I am writing about come from all walks of life, rich and poor, cultured and deprived. Unmarried mothers—and fathers—come from all kinds of backgrounds. Economics and education seem to have nothing to do with it. Most, however, have had some problem with their own parents. I have heard psychologists say that in many instances youngsters have a subconscious desire to cause a pregnancy, for revenge against neglectful parents or in rebellion against authority. In a large number of cases of illegitimacy, there has been some kind of friction between the youngsters and their parents. Often there has been discord between the parents themselves for which the youngsters are "getting even."

Some people believe the parents of sons have more responsibility than the parents of daughters for preventing illegitimacy. This theory is still another outgrowth of the old-fashioned notion that sex is all right for boys but not for girls—"No nice girl would do anything like that!" Therefore, those who believe this want fathers to exert leadership over their teen-age sons and appeal to their idealism and moral values. I agree that this should be done, but while we are at it, let us teach moral values to our daughters as well. A recent survey showed that most of those who had not engaged in sex had refrained for moral reasons. Some felt that early sex was a sign of immaturity, while those who had engaged in sex were expressing independence, loneliness, a desire to conform, or a search for a "deep commitment."

As I have said, pregnancy is often a call for help, as in the case of a teen-age college girl, the daughter of a successful businessman, who felt left out of her parents' busy social life.

When the parents were divorced, the girl blamed her father. In revenge, she began going out with a playboy her father did not like. She became pregnant, and it was not until after the baby had been placed for adoption that the girl was reconciled with her contrite father. Both had paid a high price for their new relationship.

Obesity made Jane, a high school girl, a wallflower until she went on a diet. Then the boys began to pursue her. She did not know how to handle this new-found popularity and at the age of fifteen, she became pregnant. Her overly protective family thought she was so naïve she did not know what had happened to her and they hid her in a hotel in a large city. Finally she was able to convince them she knew she was going to have a baby, and when it arrived, it was placed for adoption. In Jane's case, she could not be certain who the father was, so he was never found.

A couple I heard about recently dealt with their daughter's illegitimate child in an unusually vindictive way. They adopted the child as a "lesson" to their daughter. Everyone in the neighborhood knew the circumstances of the baby's birth, which meant that the girl's life became miserable. Boys naturally thought she was easy prey, and since she had been tagged as "a bad girl," she began meeting them secretly. It was not surprising that she became pregnant again, but this time she ran away from home and went to New York to have her baby. One of our workers found her sobbing in the dark corner of a church one Sunday morning and brought her to our Brooklyn home. We gave her shelter and helped her straighten out her life. She decided to stay with us after the baby arrived and had been adopted by a childless family in another city.

One of the most distorted senses of morality I have heard

about involved a family in a major Western city. Their daughter had an expensive society wedding although just about everyone knew she was pregnant. Neither she nor the boy wanted to get married, but they went through with an elaborate ceremony to please their parents. After the baby arrived a few months after the wedding, it was placed for adoption and the girl's family announced that it had been prematurely born dead. After a "decent" interval, the young couple were divorced.

What these three stories tell us, in addition to the fact that the parents of the young people did not do their jobs very well, is that for every teen-age pregnancy there are two troubled young people. It is gratifying to see the wonderful results when we are able to work with the boys involved as well as with the girls, and I hope that every agency and organization that gives haven to unwed mothers is making real efforts to find and help the fathers, too.

Teen-agers need a lot of guidance toward understanding that sex is part of the very meaning of life; we who work with them must help them understand this. Those who work with youth need the cooperation of parents, and this is obtained only when parents take time with their children, are frank with them, and *stop evading the issues*. Many of us tend to forget when we are confronted with a six-foot-tall fifteen-year-old boy that he may have the body of a man but the emotions of a child. We cannot treat him as a child, but we cannot trust him with a man's responsibility, either.

Parents have their jobs cut out for them. So do the churches, whose role in the rearing of moral, responsible citizens I will discuss in the next chapter.

# 10

## "God Is for Squares"

When I began this book, I said I was searching for real answers to problems of delinquency and addiction, to the reasons why some kids go wrong while others go right. Parents have borne the brunt of most of my criticisms, but the church also has been remiss, and it must share with parents the blame for the plight of many of our youth. I suspect that many people will look with disdain on my views about the role of the church in the lives of our young people. However, in nearly ten years of working with gang members and narcotics addicts, I have been able to save, or at least help, a gratifying number of youngsters. I feel I have proved many of my points in our Teen Challenge centers across the nation, in Canada, and overseas, where the same basic program is working successfully. Hundreds of life patterns have been changed, and many parents have come to us to rejoice over what we have been able to do for their children.

At this moment, I am thinking particularly of a teen-ager in Evansville, Indiana, who had a ready response when he was asked to tell how his parents had contributed to his religious education.

"Man," he declared, "my mom just doesn't dig the religion bit at all. She says God is for squares!"

The boy had been arrested for the third time on burglary charges. Before he appeared in court, I talked to him in an effort to determine how we at Teen Challenge could help him. It was clear to me that we would have to start at the beginning with this boy, but it would not be the first time we had had to do that, nor, sad to say, would it be the last. He was sentenced to jail, but we are not waiting until he comes out. Instead of arranging to have someone standing at the prison gates to greet him when he is released, we are sending visitors to see him regularly in prison. For the first time in his life, he has friends, and his attitude is changing with every visit.

This is an example of the kind of work we are increasingly being called on to do. More and more often our organization is having to step in not only to provide religious education for the delinquents with whom we work, but also to try to be substitute mothers and fathers, to give youngsters the background for life that they have not received at home or in church. We do not make an effort to be pals to kids, because we have found that that is the one thing they do not want or expect from members of the clergy, or even from our volunteers. When a minister, rabbi, or priest becomes a pal to a boy, he loses the authority and respect that are needed for a meaningful relationship. More than one youngster has said to me, "Gee, I wish he'd stop trying to be a pal to me and just try to understand my problems."

Not long ago, a series of studies was made in communities across the country on the role religion plays in the development of morals. The results were disturbingly revealing in the general attitude of teen-agers toward religion. Ninety per cent of the boys and 80 per cent of the girls said religion had no compulsive quality, and they felt that, generally, thinking in religious terms was very nebulous. They spoke of religion the way one would discuss what he was going to wear or eat tomorrow. Most of them placed the local church in the same category as the school, the drugstore, and the bowling alley. Only a scattering of youngsters were troubled at all about religious questions or problems.

It is an almost universally accepted fact that youngsters in their late teens drift away from church, perhaps never to return. This is because they have reached the age where their parents no longer require them to go to Sunday school and they make their own decisions not to go. After all, their parents don't go to church, so why should they? There is a deeper, more serious reason, too, and that is that the churches have not offered them anything they can hang on to.

There is a growing feeling among teen-agers that the church has become a kind of semiprivate club that has adapted itself mainly to the social needs of suburban families. We hear a lot about the "urban" church and ministries in slum areas, but judging from what I have seen in my slum ministry—which, by the way, I conduct not in a church with a pulpit but wherever the youngsters are—this effort on the part of Big Religion has not been an overwhelming success, to put it mildly. The storefront churches founded by many small denominations and coffeehouse chapels, such as the Catacombs Chapel my mother established on one of the worst honky-tonk streets in Greenwich Village, are more relevant to the needs of the economically depressed and educationally deprived inhabitants of our cities. They have gone to the people, while the so-called urban ministry of the major denominations mainly involves bringing the people to the church building.

You should see the young people who have straggled into the Lost Coin Chapel on Sullivan Street on week-end evenings. They have come to laugh and sneer and be served free coffee and doughnuts, but an amazing number have stayed to listen to the Gospel of love and sing folk hymns. Some of them have even ventured to thumb through the Bibles on the tables, and there is nothing my mother, Ann Wilkerson, enjoys more than an animated religious discussion with the kinds of tough-minded skeptics who have been attracted to the chapel-coffeehouse. She started her ministry to beatniks on park benches in nearby Washington Square, but when the winter weather became too rugged, she found an abandoned cellar night spot that had been called the Den of Forty Thieves and talked me into lending her some of my workers to help her fix the place up. We hung out a sign saying Catacombs Chapel, and it became one of Greenwich Village's more popular places. When the lease expired, the Lost Coin was opened a block away.

The coffeehouse ministry concept has caught on across the country. Some coffeehouses are church-sponsored, others are run independently by clergymen. They are in storefronts, church basements, and old houses. Some feature discussion groups, while others give folk music and hymn singing top billing. From what I have heard about the activities, I gather that this has been a meaningful kind of ministry that has reached young people on their own terms.

A variation of this kind of program is one of my favorite stories about religious outreach. It concerns Bill Iverson and his luncheonette. His story began on a Friday morning in his study at the First Reformed Church in Newark, New Jersey, where he was putting the finishing touches on his Sunday sermon, based on Jesus' words to Peter, "Launch out into the deep and let down your nets." Through this message, he hoped to challenge his congregation to "get out where the fish are" and bear witness for Jesus.

The more he thought about it, the more Bill realized that his message was directed at himself as much as anyone. He thought about the frustrations of his seven years in this inner-city parish where he had been unable to reach the drunks, the down-and-outers, and especially the teen-agers who milled about but never set foot in his church. He had tried to talk to alcoholics, bums, and youngsters, but they did not want to have anything to do with a minister—a "Holy Joe." They were either hostile to a clergyman or regarded him as too far removed from the realities of life to be able to discuss any down-to-earth problems.

As Bill sat mulling over his sermon, a thought flashed into his mind. He would go where the teen-agers were. And where was that? A corner luncheonette near the West Side High School, where he had seen teen-agers gathering regularly. Why not? Bill left his study immediately and drove to the place. It was still in business but had a For Sale sign in the window. Bill went in and talked with the owner. He asked if he could work for a day to see whether this would be a good way for him to reach kids. The owner agreed and put Bill to work mixing soft drinks and cooking hamburgers. Three days later, Bill bought the place.

He found it easy to start conversations over the counter, and it proved to be far more effective than sending his sermons out from the pulpit to a congregation that just sat there, perhaps not even listening. Soon Bill and the youngsters had struck up an easy relationship. They began discussing all kinds of things—school, parents, sex, drinking, dope. He did not tell them at first that he was a minister. By the time he did, it did not make any difference, because they had known him first as a friend.

Once he had become their confidant, Bill set out to make his relationship with the youngsters more constructive. He started jotting down questions to ask them and soon had a special kind of "20 Questions" game going across the counter. As soon as he felt he had the confidence of a youngster, he interviewed him and took notes. "What do you think of young people today?" "Is the world getting worse or better?" "Does life have a purpose?" "Do you believe in God?" "Is God interested in you personally?" And so on.

The teen-agers often were so flattered to have their opinions sought that they would interrupt Bill to make sure he put down their answers exactly right. "Very few grownups are interested in what we think," a Coke-sipping girl told Bill one day when he began to interview her. She told him that God was not interested in her personally, because grownups were not; to her, God was another grownup. She felt the world was getting worse, but then, she would, living over a tavern with her unmarried parents and watching her mother get drunk every day while her father worked behind the bar downstairs. She believed that Jesus rose from the dead but she had no idea why.

When the interview ended, Bill gave the girl a little book. It was the New Testament. Only two weeks later she came back and told him she had read about Jesus, and right then and there, she and Bill bowed their heads and prayed together. The next day she brought with her a friend who was to become another convert at the lunchcounter pulpit.

Bill's venture became so successful that he found himself heading week-end retreats in the mountains for teen-agers. He began counseling the parents of some of his "customers." Meanwhile, he was working toward a doctorate at New York University. He was so busy in his new ministry that he resigned his pastorate.

Unfortunately, the story did not end there. The success of this ministry almost spelled failure, for Bill eventually ran out of money. The luncheonette was a losing proposition and he had no income with which to offset business deficits. Reluctantly and sadly, Bill had to close the place. The day he locked the door, the cop on the beat almost wept and the kids wandered aimlessly about, bewildered, disappointed, and let down. But then they decided to do something. When one boy volunteered to work after school behind the counter without pay, others followed. Soon there was a sign in the window saying, "BILL'S BACK," and the place was jumping again.

Bill hopes that other ministers will try to start similar projects. "If you can have a heart-to-heart talk with a teen-ager," he says, "be honest with him, and get him to be honest with you, God can use you." He finds, as we have, that teen-agers are crying out for strong adult authority figures and grownups who will listen to them. They want to be with adults they can respect and who will give them guidance. Bill says that if you want to talk to teen-agers you have to drop your façade of adult phoniness. "If we're not real, they can't be real," he says, "and will grow up imitating the phony world—either inside or outside of the church—and missing the greatest experience life can offer, the encounter with reality which is God Himself."

The doubts and bitterness encountered by Bill Iverson at a lunchcounter are not limited to youngsters who live in the economically depressed and crowded inner city. It is not just the impoverished and underprivileged who are reacting against the church. During my frequent speech-making appearances at colleges and seminaries, I have had opportunities to talk informally with students, many of whom are bitter about the church, the clergy, and all religious institutions. A healthy skepticism is one thing, but bitterness is another.

The young people talk about the hollow social life of the church, the bait thrown out to attract new members. For example, a Dallas church boasts the largest Protestant congregation in the country and the most bowling alleys. Another large congregation is prouder of its outdoor barbecue pit and tennis courts than the content of its religious education classes. Full parking lots have become more important than overflowing pews; it's what the public sees that counts. A survey of various church activities made not long ago showed that 75 per cent of the young people who joined a particular church club did so because it offered ballroom dancing. One of New York's most fashionable churches has a waiting list of lonely people who want to join the young people's club, but there are many empty pews every Sunday.

Slowly, however, the churches are learning lessons about their role in reaching the unchurched and delinquent youth. They are discovering that programs designed only to fill social needs are almost sure to fail, for the church cannot bribe teen-agers into attendance by offering them hot dogs, pop, and dance music. One denomination has allocated nearly three million dollars for slum programs designed to reach delinquent youth through an army of professional social workers and seminary students who have been hired to conduct a social and recreational program of dances, plays, group sessions, and other activities already provided by government poverty programs.

I attended a session of about forty street workers sponsored by an interdenominational board of clergymen at which they discussed ways to reach delinquent youth in a difficult slum section in Manhattan. Here is what they outlined as a good basic program for getting through to slum kids: An all-day picnic at Jones Beach, a Shakespearean play in the basement of a church, and a street dance every Friday night. The program began, and I observed it for three nights. Not one teen-ager responded to the "challenge of the church." The slum kids were bored to death by the program and began straggling out for more exciting evenings sipping cheap wine in the cellars of deserted tenements.

This program failed because it did not meet the youngsters on their own terms. I will tell you a little later about a program we at Teen Challenge have tried, with some success, because we do not talk down to kids or try to take them out of their own milieu in order to win them to the church. We talk to them where we find them, even in the "shooting galleries" where they hide out to inject heroin into their veins.

But right now I want to tell you about the pastor of one of the larger Protestant churches in the South who flew to New York to see me. After he had read my book *The Cross and the Switchblade,* he wrote to me, disagreeing in strong words with my ideas about the role of the church in working with delinquency. "You can't get kids with straight religion," he wrote. "You have to approach them with something they like to do, like pal programming."

Now here he was in my office, apologetically seeking my advice. Here is why: He had received permission from his church board to set up a well-advertised social program in the gymnasium of the church. Word was spread through the city that gangs, dope addicts, and all youth would be welcome to attend a Saturday "bash," which would begin with a day at the beach and end with an evening of well-chaperoned social dancing in the gym. About four hundred youngsters attended, including two teen gangs, a delegation of narcotics addicts, and a number of unruly hot-rod enthusiasts. The chaperones were astonished at the wild behavior that gripped the entire group and they could not control the youngsters. By midevening, things really got out of control. Windows were splintered, furniture was smashed and cars were overturned, and the newspapers thoroughly covered what was described as a "near riot."

The program was dropped and the minister, now sadder and wiser, sat in my office and acknowledged that "the church cannot win addicts and delinquent youth through programming. It takes elements of respect, quiet dignity, and dynamic power that can be demonstrated only by preaching the Gospel of redemption."

My criticism of such church programs for youngsters extends beyond the major denominations that talk big—about money, memberships, etc. Some of the smaller evangelical churches also are out of touch with youth and are losing teenagers because of too much rigidity and insistence on conformity. Young gang members and narcotics addicts have told me they walked out of such churches when they were in their preteen years because the pastors harped only on the sins of elaborate dress, theater-going, and wearing jewelry. In some of these churches girls were required to remove jewelry before being allowed to enter. Certainly every church has a right to set standards, but when these standards drive young people away, the ministers should not cry out in alarm about the "plight" of our youth.

As an example of the Teen Challenge approach, let me tell you how three teen-age boys turned a New Jersey town upside down—or perhaps I should say rightside up. They came to my office to invite me to one of the churches in their community to speak to more than four hundred teen-agers who said they were "hungry for God." Their visit was the result of a teen-agers' riot at a swimming pool that even the police could not control. My young friends were fully committed Christians who had refused to stand idly by when the rioting began. They plunged into the melee and pulled out four or five of the troublemakers, sat them down, and began to tell them about God, Jesus, and the way religion could meet the needs of young people. In less than ten minutes the rumpus had stopped and other youngsters gathered around the three boys who were not afraid to stand by their faith. Out of their courage was born a program through which hundreds of young people were brought together every week. Some who had been considered the worst troublemakers were now praying at religious services. It was one of these meetings the three boys wanted me to address. I would not have missed the opportunity for the world.

These three boys had made the same discovery that I had

when I started preaching to gangs and delinquents in New York. Even the worst kid in a gang would listen to anyone who spoke the truth, to *him*, and would respond. I found switchblade-toting gang members willing to sit on a curbstone for a heart-to-heart talk about their spiritual needs. Never once did one of these cursing, hate-filled boys or girls turn on me or refuse to listen. One gang leader told me, "Davie, I have been sitting on this block all my seventeen years, and not one of the people who attend that church over there has ever invited me in. They just walk right past with their noses in the air as if I'm no good and I don't want God or religion. You are the first one who has ever taken the time to talk to me about God—or anything else, for that matter."

Again and again, I have heard narcotics addicts tell me about ministers who met them at the church door and refused to let them in. I nearly had it out with one slum minister for this kind of attitude. It happened when I was working with addicts on 103rd Street in Harlem and asked the pastor of a small storefront church for permission to rent his chapel one night a week so I could hold special services for addicts in their own neighborhood. He was horrified. "I don't want those bums in my church," he said. "They are no good. They cut up the seats and ruin everything. I don't want them to contaminate my church kids and my church." This was an extreme reaction, to be sure, but it is an example of the irrelevance of some of our churches.

Fox Street, in the Bronx, is another example. Known as Little Korea because of the constant warfare that goes on there, it is one of the worst areas I have ever seen. Scores of addicts live on the block and "connect" for narcotics right on the sidewalks, where little children play with litter and the contents of garbage cans. Prostitutes, pimps, drug pushers, and homosexuals live there, and as one of my boys observed, "the only decent people on the block are the alcoholics." I have preached to as many as ninety addicts at one time in street rallies in Little Korea. Our organization has rescued a number of people from the block. One of them, called Cookie, is among our missionaries now; she came from the neighborhood and has gone back to help us save others who live there.

Not long ago I escorted several minister friends through Little Korea. A church was sponsoring a street dance, and I wanted to see how this would affect the people who lived there. The street was blocked off and it was a sea of twisting, gyrating bodies, dancing to rock-and-roll music. Beer cans were flying while little children sat on the curbs and watched. The clergymen sponsors stood smiling, clapping their hands and tapping their feet in time to the music, but some of the young people in the crowd told me later they were not really having a good time. It was just "something to do" on a long, hot summer evening. They did not even know the name of the church that had sponsored the festivities.

Did the dance attract anyone to any church on Sunday? I doubt it. Did the clergymen who staged the dance learn the important lesson, that you have to take relevant church activities into the street to these people? I doubt that, too. Mere church attendance, as we all know, does not make a man religious any more than swimming turns a man into a fish. The job of the clergy is not one of making the church more appealing or offering more bribes to youth to lure it inside the door. The real task of the clergy is to acquaint itself with the heartbreak, the loneliness, the lost feeling of many youths and to engage in a simple, direct ministry of satisfying the needs of teen-agers in terms they understand.

Our courts have proved that young people cannot be expected to solve their problems by promising to turn over a new leaf or even by behaving just a little bit better. The church cannot stem the tide of immorality and save its youth by extracting promises to do better. It takes a dynamic ministry with power behind it to change the hearts and attitudes of those who accept it. Such dynamism is possible only if the clergy will speak the language of those they are approaching. One can drop ecclesiastical language and orthodox procedure without becoming one of the gang. As I have said, palship does not provide inspiration.

The Teen Challenge ministry has always been one of complete involvement on the "turf," where the kids are—on roofs, in basements, in the tenements, on the playgrounds, in the prisons. We take our message "where the action is." Our gospel message of redemption includes in-patient services where we offer beds, food, clothing, and medical care if needed, as well as a job-placement service and legal and family welfare bureaus. In our small way, we feel we are acting meaningfully and setting an example for other churches whose social action study committees recommend programs ranging from jazz masses to "handbell choirs" for slum kids. Everyone is grateful for whatever the various churches do to try to meet the problems of delinquency and neglect, but I would hope that they will eventually come to see that the bread-and-butter kinds of assistance are more productive than jazz and the ringing of handbells.

Many church-sponsored programs are relevant, of course.

In my opinion, there is no stronger force for good among young people than scouting or boys' and girls' clubs and church-sponsored ranger-type programs. Any activity that takes children into the country and close to nature is wonderful, *if religiously oriented.* Some of the delinquents we work with saw cows for the first time when we took them to a church camp. Their life patterns have been changed by their experiences of worship and Christian education and fellowship, combined with hiking, nature study, swimming, and other activities.

Not one of the addicts who has come to us has ever been a scout or a member of a church-sponsored youth program of the type I have mentioned. Such activities represent one of the greatest forces against delinquency through discipline, acceptance, interpersonal relationships, and religious education. Too often such church organizations are overlooked or merely tolerated as "tailpipe" programs. If you take any incorrigible kid, involve him in an effective church Boy Scout program, put him in uniform, pack a tent on his back, lead him on a hike through the woods until he falls exhausted at night, let him sleep under the stars, and in the morning get him up to fish for his own breakfast and then cook it—all of this under the leadership of a dedicated man who really cares about boys—I promise you he will never turn up on Teen Challenge's doorstep.

Another effective area of youth service is institutional work, an avenue open to all churches that want to devote the time to it. We need to reach the youths squandering their time in prison and those who are ill in hospitals. Teen Challenge maintains a prison department that sends teams of former addicts and gang leaders out to visit jails and hospitals to offer help, hope, and friendship to patients and inmates. Unfortunately, most churches leave jail and hospital visitations to the minister alone instead of seeking volunteers from among the congregations. Some of our best examples of rescue work have been provided by a Teen Challenge worker going to see a teenager in trouble. One visit sometimes works wonders. When the youngster gets out of jail he may come directly to us, for we were the only ones who bothered to see him when he was alone, deserted even by his family.

A person in trouble will never forget the one who cares enough to visit him when he needs a friend. The doctor, psychiatrist, and chaplain serve important functions in penal institutions, but they are a part of the establishment and are paid to do what they do. There is something special about a volunteer who goes on his own time, without pay, just to offer the hand of friendship.

Another kind of program of potential help would be regular church-sponsored services in prisons and hospitals featuring singing teams of teen-agers, down-to-earth, practical talks about religion, and followups in regular person-to-person conferences between the inmates and adults who know how to listen. I do not think it is necessary to have special training for such work. Anyone with heart can listen and love. It just takes a commitment of spirit and time.

Street work, of course, is very important to us, too. As I have emphasized, it is at the core of our Teen Challenge activities. When I approach a group of youngsters on a street corner, I know they will jeer at me if I invite them into a church. But they bow their heads with me when I lead them in prayer right there on the sidewalk. And then I stay around and listen to their gripes, their dreams, and their troubles.

I was scared stiff the first time I held a street rally in a slum block. We set up loudspeakers and floodlights while tough-looking young hoodlums stood by drinking beer and whistling at the girls from my office. Addicts lounged against lightposts and prostitutes plied their trade. I did not know what to expect, but there were moments when I feared the worst.

And then something happened. A quartet of our most inspired choir members began singing the hymn "How Great Thou Art." The activity in the street slackened. Some of the people even stopped what they were doing to listen. A few men removed their hats. I saw one drop a beer can in the gutter and stamp out his cigarette. Someone started passing a hat. After the singing, a cluster of the denizens of the block gathered around me and I told them about the Bible and Jesus and how He could change their lives. A handful of these bedraggled creatures came forward later to talk to me. They wanted to know more, and we told them more, far into the night. Former addicts were with us, as they always are on such occasions, to tell those who wanted to listen how their lives had been changed.

During such meetings, policemen usually stand by, alert for trouble, but there has not yet been an instance of violence or rowdyism during or after one of our religious meetings, as there has been at some church-sponsored dances. It makes me think that perhaps we need fewer policemen in the slums and more church men and women doing people-to-people work. Any church, large or small, any minister, trained or unskilled, can help save our future generation by reaching the young-sters. Senator Robert F. Kennedy warned not long ago that "within ten years, juvenile delinquency may be unbeatable."

I challenge the churches to beat it—now.

# 11

---

# Life *Without* Father—Exceptions to the Rule

My search for the facts behind juvenile delinquency and narcotics addiction is about ended. It has taken me into many areas, from the family, to the school, and then the church. Now it has led me back to the family again, but this time in a positive way. Throughout my search, I have heard a lot— probably more than most people—about broken homes in my work with down-and-out teen-agers. This usually means homes without fathers. By virtue of their absence, fathers often are to a large measure responsible for the sins of their sons and daughters; the father who is ineffectual because of illness, drunkenness, or sloth is charged with the blame for the delinquencies of his sons and daughters. "If there only were a strong male figure," sociologists and psychologists say, "the juvenile crime rate would plummet."

That this is true, I have not the slightest doubt. But the

quality of the mother enters very strongly into the picture, too, and nowhere can this be seen more clearly than in studying some exceptions that prove the rule. I found some notable exceptions when I came to know a number of successful men and started asking them about their upbringing. To my amazement I learned that a remarkably large proportion of them managed to rise to great heights from economically impoverished childhoods, often without fathers to help rear them or in homes where the mothers were the dominating influence.

Now I certainly am not recommending the fatherless home for any child. What I *am* saying is that the quality of the home life is not completely or necessarily dependent on the presence of both parents. The home broken by death, divorce, or illness is not always the bad home, although we certainly know that it *can* be and often is, as certainly as we know that the home with both parents in residence can be the worst—or best—of all.

My years of listening to youngsters half dead from narcotics led me to look into the role of fathers in our society. Young addicts tend to blame their broken or damaged homes for their plights. So do unwed mothers and teen-age criminals. They usually go to great lengths to tell me that they do not even know who their fathers are, that their fathers have abandoned them, or that their fathers are just plain no-good bums. Thus they feel they have explained away their delinquency.

But I was seeking a positive answer to the question of family influence on delinquency. "What better way," I asked myself, "than to try to find out what kinds of homes breed *non*delinquents?" I decided to go to the top, to seek out well-known, successful men and find out what in their upbringing helped to make them the cream of the crop. In letters to a number of these individuals, I asked them to allow me to share with you their comments on their upbringing. What was there about their home lives when *they* were growing up that provided them with that added strength that enabled them to succeed where others failed?

A gratifying number of the men replied, and at length. It turned out that quite a few began in poverty, and without fathers. Take, for example, the winners of the Horatio Alger Awards of the American Schools and Colleges Association for the single year of 1963. Charles R. Anthony, head of his own Oklahoma City corporation, was orphaned at twelve and yet managed to support himself without resorting to crime. The late Albert Dorne, president of the Famous Artists School of Westport, Connecticut, left school after the seventh grade to support his mother, two sisters, and a younger brother. Wayne A. Johnston, president of the Illinois Central Railroad, was only two when his father died, leaving his mother to support the family by teaching school.

Here is what Mr. Johnston has to say about his upbringing:

"Mother was a devoted Christian lady in the strictest sense of the word, and she believed that her three sons, one younger and one older than myself by two years each, should live their lives with due respect for a religious faith. We regularly attended, as a family, every Sunday, all of the services of the Christian Church, and as we grew older we participated in the activities of the church, such as teaching Sunday school.

"The other phase of our lives was that of accepting the circumstances in which we found ourselves (without a father) as being the plan of our Father in heaven, and accepting that it was up to us to pattern our lives so as to live similarly as did our neighbors who did not have the absence of a father. This of course required that we do everything humanly possible to assist our mother by means of working, from the time we were able to deliver newspapers until we found ourselves in positions that we would follow during the remainder of our lives.

"Thirdly, and just as important as the other two, was the fact that our mother believed in education, and even back in the early part of this century she held the position that it was not wise to do other than to have the most education that one could attain, and that of course was through college. My younger brother became assistant to the president of the University of Illinois, and was, in other words, an educator. My older brother was a legislative representative for a number of corporations. I chose railroading as my career because transportation appealed to me.

"Together with these three fundamental principles—religion, recognizing the value of work and education—was the fact that we had a mother who through her entire life demonstrated these fundamental principles. Our admiration, love and affection for her as our leader can be said to be responsible for whatever success the three of her offspring attained. In other words, what I am trying to say, most humbly, is that we believed in what we were told by our mother and did our level best to fulfill her expectations by doing the things that she indicated were important.

"Whatever success was attained by us three boys our mother deserved all the credit. I have the feeling now, as I have had throughout my entire life, that the impact of the influence of the parents on the children is the most important factor in success. As a matter of fact, I believe, and most sincerely, that a lot of the things which are detrimental to our society done by children may be traced to lack of proper interest on the part of the parents in the family life, and, might I say, the lack of love."

Another Horatio Alger winner, R. Perry Shorts, chairman of the Second National Bank of Saginaw, Michigan, who grew up without a father, also praises the strength of his mother. "My mother," he said, "was the greatest inspiration in my life. She instilled in her five children good Christian principles and impressed upon them the great importance of maintaining a good reputation so that people would trust them." Mr. Shorts's father was a small-town Methodist minister with four sons and a daughter. The father died when the oldest child was nineteen, leaving the family with no financial resources.

"Thank goodness, we were also left with the whole state of Michigan full of opportunity," Perry Shorts said. "We didn't worry about it. There were four of us boys and one girl and we all got jobs and earned as much as we could. Mother insisted that we should have good educations—and so we all went to college, one at a time—each one helping the others—and when we were all through, we had two teachers, one doctor and two lawyers in one family—and, including mother, we had six ardent boosters for American free enterprise.

"Mother always used to tell us that it wasn't so difficult to make a success in this great country—and I finally adopted a formula of my own: that if a young man lives straight and practices just three things, and sticks to it, he is bound to succeed—and those three things are thrift, hard work, and old-fashioned honesty."

W. Clement Stone, self-made multimillionaire president of

the Combined Insurance Company of America, is another
Horatio Alger winner who grew up without a father but with
a mother who had a strong personality, tremendous love for
her son, and the ability to motivate him to success.

"We were poor," he recalled not long ago, "but being poor
does not mean you have to be unhappy. I had a happy childhood.

"In fatherless homes, you often find the family is more
close-knit. Boys often grow up to have a higher regard for
womanhood because of their love for their mother."

In his book, *The Success System That Never Fails,* Mr.
Stone tells about his childhood without a father. "Even though
I was raised in a poor, run-down neighborhood, I was happy.
Aren't all children happy, regardless of poverty, if they have
a place to sleep, something to eat, and room to play?

"I lived with my mother in the home of relatives. As I
grew older, the grandfather of a girl who lived on the top
floor of our apartment building sparked my imagination with
stories of cowboys and Indians while we ate puffed rice and
milk. And each day, when he tired of his story-telling, I
would go downstairs in the backyard and live the part of
Buffalo Bill or a great Indian warrior chief. My pony, made
out of a stick or old broom, was the fastest in the West.

"Picture a working mother seeing her young son in bed
at night and asking him to tell about his day's experiences—
those that were good and those that were bad. Picture him,
after they had talked for a while, getting out of bed and
kneeling beside his mother while she prayed for guidance.
There you have the feeling of the beginning of my search for
the true riches in life."

Young Clem's mother became concerned because he had

begun to keep "bad company" and smoked cigarettes he rolled himself. He played hookey from school, too. Fortunately he had confidence enough in his mother to tell her about it. She prayed for guidance in dealing with this situation and found the solution in sending her son to a parochial boarding school so he could be exposed to a wholesome environment. There the boy developed a secret ambition to be like the pastor he most loved and admired. "But I also loved my mother, and I missed her very much," he related. "Like so many boys living away from home at private schools, I was homesick, and like them, every time I saw my mother or wrote to her, I would beg her to bring me home permanently." After two years, Mrs. Stone sent for her boy. She began a successful business career, eventually entering the insurance field, and this inspired young Clem to go into insurance, too. With his mother's inspiration and $100, he built one of the nation's largest accident and health insurance companies. He also put his wealth to work helping other people, particularly young people.

He says today that religion was one of the chief factors in his success, and he owes this to his mother. "I don't care what the religion is," he declares, "there must be a good religious environment. With a strong religious influence, it is possible for a boy to learn to say 'No' when his friends want to do something they should not."

Discipline is another factor. "If a parent really loves a youngster, he learns to *discipline himself* to have the courage to say 'No' to him when he should instead of giving in. My mother had that courage, I am happy to say."

As the child of a working mother, young Clem had to learn to say "No" too. He had a great deal of freedom and thus had

to make many of his own decisions. "Because I was independent and took the teachings of the church seriously," he recalls,
"I had the courage to do what I thought was right regardless of
my associates." As a result, no matter where he was, even at
Boy Scout camp, after the other boys had gone to bed, he
would kneel down and pray before climbing into his bunk,
even though admittedly "I didn't like the idea on a cold
night."

There have been others who have succeeded in life despite
the fact they did not have fathers. Dr. Abner Vernon McCall,
president of Baylor University, was only three when his father
died. Later, when his mother became too ill to support her
four children, they were placed in a Masonic home. Yet
McCall was motivated to win a scholarship to the university
he now heads. Because his father was an invalid, John W.
Rollins, president of the Rollins Leasing Corporation, had to
help with Georgia farm chores. Instead of being embittered by
this, he went on to lead a good, constructive life.

Just to give you a few more brief examples, earlier Horatio
Alger Award winners included William G. Karnes, president
of the Beatrice Foods Company, who was orphaned at five
and was reared by two aunts. A mining accident disabled the
father of Merl C. Kelce, president of the Peabody Coal Company, when he was seven, and he and his brothers picked
strawberries to help support the family. C. R. Smith, president
of American Airlines, worked as a youth in Texas to help
support his mother and six brothers and sisters. The present
board chairman of Bausch & Lomb, Carl S. Hallauer, was
orphaned at the age of nine and supported himself selling
newspapers. Ed Leach, president of the Jack Tar Hotels, lost
his father at twelve; he was additionally handicapped by club

feet, which were so successfully corrected in a number of operations that he won admission to West Point. Adolph Zukor was a ragged, sixteen-year-old orphan when he arrived in the United States from Hungary with only forty dollars sewn in the lining of his coat. He became one of Hollywood's most successful movie figures.

And let us not forget our most illustrious orphan, President Herbert Hoover, who lost both parents when he was seven. Mr. Hoover went to college and became a phenomenally successful engineer before he began to devote his life to the humanitarian pursuits that led him to the Presidency.

That is a rather impressive array of fatherless—and in some instances also motherless—men who have acquitted themselves well, made fortunes in most cases, and devoted considerable time, effort, and money to helping others. The chief influence in their childhoods, for the most part, that helped them succeed as human beings appears to have been the presence of a strong figure who guided them along religious, moral, and educational paths. And there also was lots of love in the lives of most of these men.

# 12

---

# They Are YOUR Kids,
# Wrong—or Right!

It is unlikely that there will ever be a real end to my search for
the truth about why kids go wrong—or right, but I have
reached a point where I can draw a number of conclusions
and pass some of my thinking along to other parents. First I
would like to ask several questions.

What kind of parent are *you?* What kind of children are
*you* rearing? Are your kids among the 95 per cent of American
youngsters who are members of the upbeat generation, whose
exploits are reported on honor rolls and in school publications? Or, are they among the delinquent 5 per cent whose
names are on police blotters and who are included in national
crime statistics, who attract a disproportionate amount of
attention in newspaper headlines and require enormous ex-
penditures of time and money?

I am grateful to J. Edgar Hoover for reminding us that basically most of our youngsters are honest, and except for those with mental deficiencies, appear to know the basic difference between right and wrong. But we still have the "5 per centers" to plague those who are in the 95 per cent bracket. Just glancing at the bare statistics, you might be justified in wondering why there should be so much noise about juvenile delinquency. But if you search further, you will find that federal, state and local governments, church organizations, schools, and private bodies devote millions of dollars a year and countless man-hours to coping with the 5 per cent, all at the expense of the 95 per cent.

You have accompanied me on my search for clues to why some of our kids go wrong while others go right. Out of this search the six basic essentials of good parenthood have become clear, at least to me: love, supervision, discipline, communication, companionship, and religious education. And it seems that if you love your children and can communicate with them, the other qualities that constitute good parenthood will just come naturally.

A recently published study by a prominent psychiatrist showed dramatically that 77 per cent of all our problem children come from families without adult supervision, which really means without love. Most of the reports I have read on delinquency by psychologists and sociologists point to a lack of proper communication between parents and children, and therefore also the absence of love.

Few youngsters I have worked with have ever known what it meant to have parents who were really involved in their lives. Their fathers never played ball with them. Their mothers did not bake cookies or cakes for them or make lemonade on hot summer days. PTA meetings were shunned. Sunday was a time for individual pursuits. Mealtimes were not occasions for families to sit down together and talk, but rather ordeals to be rushed through in a hurry. Nobody cared what Jimmy or Susie did after school as long as they were out of the way. There was little interest in progress in school. These youngsters were, for the most part, left alone to shift for themselves. It amazes me when I think of the number of children from homes such as these who somehow have managed to turn out all right. And I have been astonished also when I have seen financially solid homes run just as haphazardly as some of our tenement dwellings.

Most of the youngsters who have turned up at Teen Challenge have gone bad because their parents appeared to be unconcerned about which way they were going in life. Deprived children go wrong. So do children from advantaged homes, but often for different reasons. Too much pressure and over-planning do as much harm to the suburban youth as neglect does to the poor kid in the city.

On learning his child is in trouble, the suburban parent says, "I can't figure it out. We did everything for our child." This parent saw to it that every minute of his children's day was occupied—school, music lessons, dancing lessons, little league sports, club meetings, and tutoring sessions to make sure he got into college. Mom has been the chauffeur, carrying the kids from one activity to another. The parents are in a rat race for status in their community and they have thrust their children into a mouse race, herding, goading, and pressuring their youngsters to be popular, to be successful, to get into the right college. These children are being suffocated, but not by love. With loving concern and communication, the pressures that prompt some kids to steal, smoke marijuana, get drunk, or seek an outlet in illicit sex would not be there.

We parents must learn to be involved in the lives of our children without becoming too involved, without smothering and frustrating them. We have to judge when to withdraw from their activities and stand aside and let nature take its course. We need to allow for personal development and initiative. Children have a way of turning out all right when they are given a chance to explore their own world as long as they are within reach and sound of their loving mothers and fathers.

I learned from my own son that you can go too far in trying to be a pal to your kids. Last summer I decided that I should spend more time with Gary, who was then eight, so I invited him to go bicycle riding with me on three consecutive days. On the third day, after we had ridden about two miles, he pulled off the road and flopped down on the ground.

"How are you doing, pal?" I asked.

"O.K., Daddy, but are you sure you aren't tired?"

I knew something was "bugging" him, so I dug a little deeper. Eventually he looked embarrassed and blurted it out.

"I've been going with you just so you'd know I still love you," Gary said.

It turned out that he would have preferred to be playing with his friends. You should have seen the expression of relief that swept his face when we started home so he could join his neighborhood pals, who were building a tree house. Now Gary and I spend most of each Monday afternoon together. Both of us plan for it. His friends and my associates know that it is Dad's day and we are comfortable together. The rest of the week, both of us are too busy to spend much time together, but it does not matter because Monday is our day.

This is one path to communication between parent and child, but there are others. In our home, and in the homes of a few others I know, parents are always available to answer their children's questions and to talk to them. We encourage them to do their homework, but without ever actually helping them do it. We try to make our dinner table conversation an occasion for a real exchange of ideas. The children, my wife, and I save interesting experiences or problems concerning us all to discuss at the table, and each has his chance to talk. This I find is a rarity in our busy society where everyone is in such a hurry to get to the next order of business of the day that meals are bolted in silence or are the occasion for family fights.

Rules for child-rearing are easy to come by, but I do feel deeply that there are some that are intelligent guidelines for family living. Before I present these ideas on how to help your kids grow up, however, let me pass on to you a few of the comments I have heard from teen-agers who have talked to me after hearing me speak at meetings.

During a recent tour of the larger cities in England, I had a chance to talk to teen-agers and I learned that youngsters on the other side of the Atlantic have much the same concerns and problems as ours do. Parents everywhere seem to be basically the same, and so are the youngsters.

Here is what a sixteen-year-old boy told me in Bristol: "My folks are good people, but they just aren't with it. They don't know what I have to be to keep up with the crowd, so I'm really two people. They know just one side of me, but they seem satisfied with that. It's easy to fool them."

John, a teen-ager, took me for a walk through Soho, London's counterpart of Greenwich Village. "See all those strip joints?" he observed. "That's where our fathers go for entertainment. Then they go home and lecture to us about bad women. It takes a stupid kid to fall for mockery like that. We've got eyes. Parents should set the right example or keep quiet."

Thousands of miles away, in Los Angeles, a fifteen-year-old girl told me: "If being interested is communication, I'd say my parents do communicate. There are a thousand ways they show their interest. But they let me choose my own religion and faith instead of offering guidance and then regulate my meals and tell me what brand of toothpaste to use. My mother is afraid I will get too emotional about religion, but she sobs over the soap operas on television. It just doesn't add up."

Another California teen-ager came to me to tell me she was pregnant. "My folks are sick about it. They think that sex education should have been enough to keep me from getting hung up on a boy. They have always been more worried about me having a baby than about my knowing what real love means. I learned the hard way about the difference between love and lust. I don't think my mother knows how to reach me with sex values."

A nineteen-year-old narcotics addict who lives in Brooklyn told me how he had been looking in on life from the outside since early childhood. "I remember standing outside Yankee Stadium two years ago and watching all the dads and their kids getting in their cars," he said. "I was high on 'stuff,' but I still remember how I hurt. It wouldn't have taken a ball game to grab me. All it would have taken was a swift kick in the pants or a slap on my face. I wanted someone to really care what happened to me. I don't understand the question about communication and all that, but I understand what it means to sit all night in a cold subway with no one to tell you to come or go, and no one to talk to with respect. . . ."

A fifteen-year-old minister's daughter had this to say: "I think parents want to be in the dark about certain things. Take me, for instance. My dad's a minister and I think he knows I go to Greenwich Village every Friday night. I tell him I'm staying with friends, but he knows I'm running around with two beatniks. He takes me shopping, just to talk, but he never comes right out with it about what I'm doing. He told me he didn't like my long hair but it was up to me to make the choice.

"I've lost my faith. I'm really an atheist in my heart and I'm dropping out of school. My father could have stopped me, but he was afraid he would make me bitter. I know he is really worried about me, and so am I, but I don't know what to do."

A Houston, Texas, minister's son has rebelled by refusing to cut his shoulder-length hair and wear conventional clothes. "My dad says I am incorrigible," he said. "The last time we talked we almost had a fist fight. He traveled for the first seven years of my life and I hardly knew he was alive. Now, all of a sudden, he won't let me breathe without a license.

"My mother just cries and begs me to be good. I'm not really bad. I'm just trying to show them they can't shove me around for no reason at all. When I was twelve I wanted a father I could talk to, but he was never there. Now that I've got my own friends and do a little drinking, he wants to have a heart-to-heart talk with me. It is too late and he knows it, so he's trying to get me to go to Chicago to live with my uncle.

That way I won't be an embarrassment to him any more. I'll be out of his way."

Just so no one will think that all children have these problems, let me tell you what a seventeen-year-old Boston boy said. "My dad is an advertising executive and I've got it pretty nice," he told me. "I think I'm well adjusted and I've never been bored. Both Mom and Dad are always busy and I spend summers away from them. I think I'll make it because Dad has always been a friend, not just a father, but a real friend. We talk."

Perhaps an effective way for me to spell out some guidelines on rearing children to go right instead of wrong would be first to use a little reverse psychology and outline ten ways to produce a juvenile delinquent:

1. *Keep your children out of sight and silent.* Stop their eternal questions and pestering for attention. Turn away their important queries by saying, "You're too young to know," or "Don't bother me with that now." Repress them when they act their age in childish ways.

2. *Hound them to be at the top of their class in school.* Tell them they *have* to go to college whether they want to or not. Make a scene whenever they bring home unsatisfactory report cards. Never compliment them on the best work they do; just pick on the poor results. Make sure they feel they are stupid and lazy if they don't make all A's and B's. Put the pressure on them.

3. *If you cannot or do not take your children to church, don't bother to send them.* Use the excuse that they are too young to understand about God or the church. Tell them to wait until they are old enough to make up their own minds.

Don't let your day of rest be disturbed by having to send your children off to Sunday school.

4. *Have your fights in front of your children.* Make certain they see and hear everything. Pick on each other within the family circle but be sure to act affectionately toward one another when company comes so that your children will come to know you as phonies, a knowledge that will adversely affect them all the rest of their lives.

5. *Don't be too interested in your children's friends.* Let them run around with any kids they choose. Take the attitude that if some of their friends are undesirable, your boy or girl will be a good influence on them. Do not be firm about your children's associates and do not make sure that you know at all times where the youngsters are and what they are doing.

6. *Demonstrate your love for your children with material things.* Fill their pockets with money. Let them buy all the clothes they want. Make sure they get the impression that they do not need to turn to stealing for the things they want because you will give them everything you can. Give your child the things you could not have when you were growing up and then when he gets in trouble you will be able to tell yourself, "There isn't a thing I haven't given that child! I cannot understand why he had to steal."

7. *Set a bad example so the children will not want to grow up to be like you!* When a father gets drunk periodically, the mother should warn her children against growing up like "the old man." A father should point out to his daughters he hopes they won't turn out the way their mother has—a poor housekeeper and disinterested cook. Cheat a little on your income tax and violate the speed laws and then bawl the kids out whenever they tell a lie or crib in a school examination.

8. *Refuse to believe it when you are told your children have done something wrong.* Stand up to their teachers when they complain and tell them they must be mistaken. When Junior comes home with a bloody nose, go out and berate his adversary's father without finding out who was to blame for the fight. If you fight your child's battles for him, he may reward you some day with the honor of standing beside him in juvenile court.

9. *Don't be too tough in disciplining your children, lest they hate you for it.* Ignore their temper tantrums. Never spank them. Bribe them into obedience by threatening to cut down allowances or reduce television time. If that makes them angry, tell them they are acting like delinquents. If you fail to keep threats of punishment they will learn your bark is worse than your bite and become incorrigible.

10. *Never discuss the facts of life with your children.* Let them learn about sex from their playmates and from pornographic literature they buy or borrow and sneak into the house. Put a taboo on discussions about sex in the home. Let them learn with a little experimenting and then overlook their transgressions. Don't be concerned as long as they know how to keep from having babies. Ignore talk about drug addiction and delinquency as exaggerations and things that never could involve your children.

Follow these rules and your kids are likely candidates to qualify for the delinquent 5 per cent. Violate the rules and your chances are high of having decent, upbeat kids.

Teen-agers themselves have given me some positive tips on how to give your kids a chance, and I would like to pass them on to you. In the language of the youngsters themselves, it is colorful jargon indeed, but quite to the point, as you will see:

1. *"Keep your cool."* Don't lose your temper in every crisis. Don't get excited when things go wrong. Kids need the confidence only a steady hand and settled soul can offer.

2. *"Don't get hung up on a jag that keeps you away from home."* Salesmen fathers should keep in touch with their families somehow. Mothers should forego heavy social schedules to be at home to supervise the children. If a mother works, she should make sure someone else is on hand.

3. *"Don't get strung out."* Stay away from liquor and sleeping pills. Be a square.

4. *"Bug me a little."* Use strict but loving discipline. Show your kids who is boss. Don't just let them ride out the storms. Help them anchor their ships.

5. *"Don't blow your class."* Keep the dignity of parenthood. Stay on a pedestal, if your children have put you there. Don't dress, act, and swing the way teen-agers do. Let them know you are an adult.

6. *"Light me a candle."* Show your children the way to faith. Tell them that God is not dead, sleeping, hiding—or on vacation. Give them the security of a living faith.

7. *"Take the world off my shoulders."* Share your children's problems. Discuss morals, life and love, eternity, beauty, peace of mind, and values with them. Try to help them understand that the world can be a good place in which to achieve.

8. *"Scare the hell out of me."* When you catch a child in his first encounter with smoking, drinking, or sex, punish him. Let him know why you are taking punitive action and impress upon him that more stringent measures will be taken if the transgression is repeated. Be certain he understands what he has done wrong and why it is wrong and that you are doing

this out of love and concern and not to be vindictive. By all means, do not mete out punishment in anger.

9. *"Call my bluff."* Let a youngster know once and for all that you mean what you say. Regardless of what threats a teen-ager makes—to run away, to become a delinquent, to drop out of school—stand firm and the bluffing will cease.

10. *"Be honest with me."* Always tell your children the truth. Never keep them in doubt where you stand on any matter. Be truthful and generous in praise, and then when it comes time to criticize, they will believe you and respect your judgment.

The do's and don'ts are simple to describe but they can be difficult to carry out. However, every child, as well as every adult, needs limits and rules to live by. The teen-ager especially craves reassurance that his parents are interested enough to try to keep him from getting into trouble. And all youngsters need discipline that will enable them to direct their energies into creative channels. All of us have developed behavior patterns based on the behavior patterns of those who cared for us as children. We, in turn, are providing our children with their behavior patterns.

Rather than dwelling further on this subject, perhaps we should all pause now and take stock of ourselves. What are we as parents doing to contribute to the development of healthy patterns? What are we doing that may hurt our children? How can we become better parents so we can help our kids to grow up, so we can give them a chance to go right instead of wrong?

You may find your answer sooner than you realize. You may find it in the expression on your child's face and the sound of his voice when you greet him at breakfast tomorrow morning with a kiss or a hug or a pat on the back.

## DATE DUE

| | | | |
|---|---|---|---|
| NOV 14 '68 | DEC 12 '68 | APR 30 '75 | FEB 26 '76 |
| JAN 18 '69 | JAN 14 '69 | MAR 4 '77 | FEB 26 '77 |
| JAN 18 '69 | FEB 4 '69 | | |
| MAR 4 '69 | FEB 25 '69 | MAY 2 '77 | MAY 2 '77 |
| OCT 28 '69 | OCT 22 '69 | DEC 12 '79 | DEC 12 '79 |
| NOV 8 '69 | NOV 3 '69 | AP 12 '83 | MAR 29 '83 |
| DEC 17 '69 | DEC 17 '69 | MY 02 '86 | MAY 5 '88 |
| JAN 12 '70 | JAN 12 '70 | AP 20 '88 | APR 11 '88 |
| MAY 28 '71 | MAY 14 '71 | | |
| FEB 13 '72 | FEB 3 '72 | | |
| APR 19 '72 | APR 24 '72 | | |
| MAY 16 '72 | MAY 14 '72 | | |
| JUN 22 '72 | | | |
| | JUN 22 '72 | | |
| | JUN 7 '73 | | |
| JUN 21 '73 | JUN 26 '73 | | |
| FEB 10 '75 | FEB 10 '75 | | |
| MAR 3 '75 | MAR 3 '75 | | |
| MAR 19 '75 | MAR 19 '75 | | |
| GAYLORD | | | PRINTED IN U.S.A. |